Illustrations by Vern Scharf

TOTAL MIND POWER

How to use
the other 90%
of your mind.

Donald L. Wilson, M.D.

ARROW BOOKS

ARROW BOOKS

Arrow Books Ltd
3 Fitzroy Square, London W1P 6JD

An imprint of the Hutchinson Publishing Group

London Melbourne Sydney Auckland Wellington
Johannesburg and agencies throughout the world

First published by Arrow Books Ltd 1979
© Camaro Publishing Company 1976
Printed and bound by Times Printers, Singapore.
ISBN 0 09 920440 1

This book is
dedicated
to everyone.

AUTHOR'S NOTE

This book is meant to be read throughout, from cover to cover. Technical, medical, and scientific words have been purposely simplified or omitted so that it may be used by everyone in an easy and straightforward way. Each chapter adds new ideas to be used with the step-by-step methods described.

You will be able to use the tremendous powers of your mind immediately after you read this book from front to back.

CONTENTS

INTRODUCTION

The mind undoubtedly is one of the most powerful tools mankind has to work with, yet so much of its potential has remained neglected. In fact, scientists estimate that we use only about 10 percent of our minds, leaving 90 percent untapped. In this book I want to show you how to use your Total Mind Power so you can reach whatever goal you seek, as well as help you develop better physically and mentally.

The principles of Total Mind Power are not new, but for the first time they are explained in this book for you to use. Until now, information about how the mind works has for the most part been hidden in medical libraries and in research center bookshelves. I have taken the research and documented materials out of the laboratories, and put them into a form that can help the general public: anyone concerned with better health and a better life.

Over the years I have used Total Mind Power on myself, patients, and friends. Medical colleagues have asked me how they may apply it in their professional practice. This book has been written partly to answer

that need and also, and perhaps even more import-
antly, to give each person the knowledge that will
help him use the techniques of Total Mind Power
for his own benefit.

Total Mind Power is not religiously oriented. You
don't have to join any group or cult, pay membership
fees or shut yourself off from society. Rather, Total
Mind Power requires only that you believe in the
existence of the vast—90 percent—untapped mental
resources that are available in all of us.

Total Mind Power requires a faith in ourselves, in
a potential we all have but which has been disregarded
all these years. It is not in conflict with the world
about you, but rather will provide you the abilities
to live in it better and to enjoy life more.

There are no drugs, pills, long sessions of concentration or meditation, study courses or any of the
other trappings that have been popularized by the
numerous cults and mystic philosophies that have
tried to offer panaceas for human problems. Total
Mind Power relies on you to use your own mind to
resolve your own specific problems and improve
your own self. You direct your mind toward your
specific need.

What Total Mind Power does is give you access
to the vast reservoir of your mind and then show you
how to activate it so it can work for you. This great
potential has always been with you but because of
numerous factors, including the influence of our
education, society's demands and pressures, and the
fact that information about Total Mind Power has
been hidden in documents and books, we have lacked
knowledge of this precious tool that can help us
accomplish so much.

Yet Total Mind Power is not supernatural but a
supremely natural way of making the maximum use
of the mind—the 90 percent that too often lies dor-
mant during most peoples' lives. This book provides

the key to opening the door to the fullest use of your mind.

This book is for those who are ready to use their minds completely for the first time as well as those who have tried to solve their problems by themselves or with outside assistance from friends, counselors and professionals only to be disappointed, even after spending much time, effort, and money.

The solution to your problems is free once you have learned the techniques and gained access to your own total mind. Total Mind Power will work for you. All you have to do is apply the information and techniques described in this book. They are proved procedures that have worked for many and will work for you.

Donald L. Wilson, M.D.

Donald L. Wilson, M.D.
San Francisco

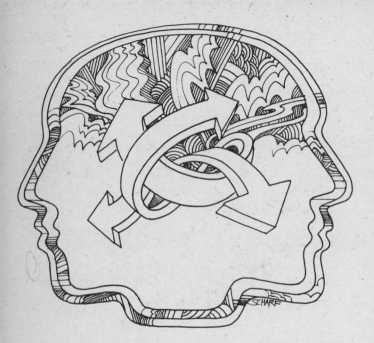

CHAPTER 1:
WHAT THIS BOOK WILL SHOW YOU.

The mind is a remarkable instrument. It is a great collector and storer of information, as well as the controller of our physical and mental functions. The 90 percent of the mind that is not put to use daily can be tapped for a healthier life whether it be for better physical stamina and health, an improved memory, reduction of tensions, a positive attitude in the tackling of problems, or improvement on the tennis court.

To achieve these goals using Total Mind Power, we shall refer to the mind's functions as using 10 percent and using the other 90 percent. 10 percent is the conscious-functioning part used for our everyday experiences such as touching, seeing, and feeling.

The untapped 90 percent is the portion of the mind we are concerned with making use of to help us attain good health and a good life.

KNOWLEDGE ABOUT THE MIND HAS UNDERGONE A LONG DEVELOPMENT. Most of the current information about the mind is contained in scientific and medical journals. This information is often difficult to bring together in usable form, and therefore is not readily available. Therefore many important advances in the use of our minds remain unrevealed. It took more than 10 years for penicillin to be used for the public after it was discovered, 20 years for television's principles to be implemented on a broad scale and 100 years for the basic computer inventions to be put to use. The use of the other 90 percent of our mind has followed a similar path.

BUT NOW THE BENEFITS OF USING YOUR MIND IN CERTAIN WAYS ARE BECOMING MORE GENERALLY KNOWN AND ACCEPTED BY SCIENTISTS AND DOCTORS. The knowledge of Total Mind Power has been gathered and synthesized in a usable form and combined with practical applications—to permit everyone to reach their full potentials in all areas of life.

I genuinely hope my efforts in bringing together the research and studies in the practical applications of the use of the mind will benefit you in the many ways it has helped me and my patients to lead fuller and healthier lives.

SIMPLE STEPS TO BE TAKEN. To draw power from the 90 percent of our minds—that waits to be tapped—there are three simple steps. Step One is to allow the mind to drift easily and freely into a state of focused awareness that is different from everyday awareness.

Step Two is to direct the mind in a specific direction to work for you in a specific way.

Step Three is to direct the mind in the sequence that will achieve and maintain your goals.

The details of these steps are covered in Chapter 7.

TOTAL MIND POWER'S TECHNIQUES ARE BENE-
FICIAL IN OUR TOTAL LIFE. Good health is only half
the story of Total Mind Power. It can also be used
with great effect to produce beautiful dreams, improve
your creative potential, better your sports performance
and improve many other areas of your life that are
discussed in later chapters.

What is common to all these areas of your health
and life's activities is that they are all related to and
influenced by your mind. You probably have heard
of psychosomatic illnesses. Examples of such illnesses
fill medical literature, ranging from stomach ulcers to
migraine headaches and nervous conditions. Each of
these is an example of the mind's influence on bodily
functions. Many of these illnesses can be eliminated or
at least greatly diminished by using Total Mind Power.

HOW ARE DOCTORS USING MIND TECHNIQUES?
Many doctors are starting to instruct their patients
in using their minds to alleviate their diseases, but a
variety of techniques are used and are often confusing
and impractical to the patient. They range from hypnosis to sensory isolation, meditation, task motivation
instructions, relaxation procedures, biofeedback, yoga,
and many more. All these techniques have features
in common relating to the mind. This book will show
you how to put together the best features from all of
these techniques as well as additional techniques found
in scientific and medical journals. The Total Mind
Power techniques are simple and easy to use.

TOTAL MIND POWER AND MEDICAL ATTENTION
GO TOGETHER. A special benefit of Total Mind Power techniques is that they can be used along with your
doctor's treatments. Medical research has shown that
when patients take an active role in using their minds

to alleviate their illnesses, they tend to get well faster. And there is no conflict between using your mind to get better and using your doctor's care—they complement each other for achieving good health.

WARNING: DON'T FORGET TO SEE YOUR DOCTOR FOR PROPER MEDICAL ATTENTION. Although Total Mind Power techniques can be used and applied to all your mental and physical health problems, they are not intended to replace the care and treatment of your doctor. If you have a health problem it is best to seek your doctor's advice and care. And then along with his treatments, use Total Mind Power techniques to speed the recovery process. Explain to your doctor your plans for using Total Mind Power and how you want to use the full power of your mind to aid in the resolving of the problem. He should be pleased to learn of your intentions. And discussing your problems with him will lead to gaining further ideas about them. As we will see in later chapters, more knowledge about your problem can be useful in applying Total Mind Power because it enables you to visualize the solution—a key to using your mind for problem resolution.

TOTAL MIND POWER IS A HEALTHY AND NATURAL APPROACH TO A GOOD LIFE. One distinguishing feature of Total Mind Power is its gentle approach to the use of your mind in harmony with your nature, to bring out the natural capabilities and powers of your mind. The techniques are complete in this book and include examples you can tailor to your specific needs. Total Mind Power is a healthy habit to acquire for all your needs—for good health and a good life.

REFERENCES

Bandura, A., "Principles of Behavior Modification." New York: Holt, Rinehart & Winston, 1969.

Berne, E., "Games People Play." New York: Grove Press, Inc., 1964.

Brody, M.W., Prognosis and Results of Psychoanalysis. In J.H. Nodine and J.H. Moyer (eds.) "Psychosomatic Medicine." Philadelphia: Lea and Febiger, 1962.

Crider, D.B., Cybernetics: A Review of What it Means and Some of its Applications to Psychiatry. "Neuropsychiatry, 1956-57, 4:35-38.

Dean, S.R., Is There an Ultraconscious Beyond the Unconscious?, "Canadian Psychiatric Association Journal," 1970, 15:57-61.

Denny, D., Modeling Effects Upon Conceptual Style and Cognitive Tempo. "Child Development," 1972, 43:105-419.

Eysenck, H.J., "Uses and Abuses of Psychology," London: Penguin Books, 1953.

Freud, S., "The Standard Edition of the Complete Works of Sigmund Freud." London: Hogarth Press, 1964.

Haley, J., "Uncommon Therapy: The Psychiatric Techniques of Milton H. Erickson, M.D.," New York: Norton & Co., 1973.

Huxley, A., "The Doors of Perception." New York: Harper & Row, 1954.

Jones, E., "The Life and Works of Sigmund Freud. Vol. I, II, III." New York: Basic Books, 1955.

Kanfer, F.H. and Karoly, P., Self-regulation and its Clinical Application: Some Additional Conceptualizations. In R.C. Johnson, P.R. Dolecki and O.H. Mowrer, "Conscience, Contract and Social Reality," 1972, 428-438.

Jung, C.G., "Man and His Symbols." Garden City: Doubleday and Co., 1968.

Ornstein, R.E., "The Psychology of Consciousness." San Francisco: W.H. Freeman and Co., 1972.

Sargent, W., "Battle for the Mind." New York: Doubleday and Co., 1957.

Szasz, T.S., "The Myth of Mental Illness." New York: Harper and Row Publishers, 1974.

Thompson, R.F., Patterson, M.M. and Teyler, T.J., The Neurophysiology of Learning. "Annual Review of Psychology," 1972, 23:73-104.

CHAPTER 2:
TOTAL MIND POWER—IT WILL MEET YOUR
EVERY NEED AND CHANGE YOUR LIFE.

USING TOTAL MIND POWER IS A NATURAL PROCESS.
It requires no pills, drugs, stimulants or depressants,
sounds, chants, psychedelic lighting. It requires only
you and your mind and the desire to tap it for the
benefits you seek.

TOTAL MIND POWER COSTS NO MONEY. This book
is all you need to learn how to use Total Mind Power
so it can benefit you. There are no groups to join,
no devices to buy, no counselors or instructors to pay.

TOTAL MIND POWER OFFERS IMMEDIATE RESULTS.
After reading this book and applying the techniques,
you will often find the solution to a situation immediately. Total Mind Power does not normally involve
a long-term process but rather provides a swift but
effective method for overwhelming obstacles.

TOTAL MIND POWER CAN BE USED ANYWHERE,
ANY TIME. Your mind accompanies you wherever you
go; it is not excess baggage. So whenever something
disturbs you or you have a goal to attain, Total Mind
Power is available.

TOTAL MIND POWER AIDS MEDICAL ATTENTION. As stated earlier, Total Mind Power is not meant to replace professional medical attention. Some physicians have suggested certain mind techniques to their patients to help them, along with the medical attention they are receiving, in the relief of pain and in general to diminish the effects of the illness being treated. Total Mind Power provides the doctor with more practical and concise techniques to offer his or her patients.

TOTAL MIND POWER REQUIRES NO TRAINING. You don't have to attend sessions or lectures to learn how to use Total Mind Power. You teach yourself with the reading of this book and the use of its techniques. This book will show you how to tap that 90 percent of your mind and use its resources to help you with any situation, or to attain the goals you seek. Total Mind Power incorporates simple and straightforward techniques and requires no degrees, no classroom attendance and no outside help, just *you*.

IF DESIRED, TOTAL MIND POWER CAN BE DONE IN GROUPS. While Total Mind Power is applied on an individual basis, its techniques also can be applied by groups who have a common problem, such as stopping smoking or losing weight. Individuals in groups formed for these purposes receive all the benefits of Total Mind Power and have the added benefit of meeting and socializing with their friends. The important thing to remember is that for an individual or in numbers, Total Mind Power works.

TOTAL MIND POWER IS COMPATIBLE WITH ANY FAITH, BELIEF, OR THERAPY. Unlike other techniques that require you to be a "follower" of a certain sect or group, observe its rituals, sing its chants, or worship its founders or leaders, Total Mind Power is not religious-ly oriented or associated with any belief or faith. Rather it is compatible with any belief you may have, because all it requires is for you to have faith in your own mind and its ability to help you.

ALTERNATIVES TO TOTAL MIND POWER CAN BE IMPRACTICAL AND EXPENSIVE. Some require constant meditation, others demand performance of certain rit-uals at fixed times each day and for prolonged periods. With Total Mind Power, once you have learned the sim-ple techniques you will find it possible to use them any time the need arises, rather than at some fixed schedule. Your needs are what will remind you when to use them. You don't forget Total Mind Power because it is always with you, handy, free and ready to use to solve your problems.

TOTAL MIND POWER TECHNIQUES ARE NOT FORCED, BUT PLEASANT TO USE. The techniques of Total Mind Power may be conducted in any surrounding that fits your circumstances. It could be a quiet part of your home, a green field, a seat on the subway, at your of-fice or in the dentist's chair. They are easy and enjoy-able to apply and you will feel assured that they will make your problems drift away.

TOTAL MIND POWER IS SELF-DIRECTED. There are no outside figures or personalities. You use a natural gift, your mind, to find relief from difficult situations and help improve your well-being, both physically and emotionally. What is remarkable about Total Mind Pow-er is that you are in complete control of its application, contents and directions. There are *no outside influences*, and the techniques are safe and leave no harmful side effects.

TOTAL MIND POWER IS WITH YOU FOR LIFE. This book is written not only to help you overcome the immediate causes of your problems, but to provide you with a lifelong way of keeping them from recurring. Also, the techniques of Total Mind Power are always with you, so they can be called upon to meet any situation. They are your companions for life and will help make life more promising and rewarding.

Chasing fads or some momentary contrivance is not the answer. Total Mind Power is as lasting as you are. The results of its use will convince you of its lifelong value and I am convinced it will lead you to a fuller and more enriched life.

REFERENCES

Gelhorn, E., "Principles of Autonomic-Somatic Interactions." Minneapolis: University of Minnesota Press, 1967.

Green, E., Green, A. and Walters, D., "Voluntary Control of Internal States: Psychological and Physiological. "Journal of Transpersonal Psychology," 1970, 1:1-26.

Haley, J. (ed.), "Advanced Techniques of Hypnosis and Therapy: Selected Papers of Milton H. Erickson." New York: Grune and Stratton, 1967.

Hartland, J., "Medical and Dental Hypnosis." Baltimore: The Williams and Wilkins Co., 1973.

Kroger, W.S., "Clinical and Experimental Hypnosis in Medicine, Dentistry and Psychology." Philadelphia: J.B. Lippincott Co., 1963.

Perls, F.S., "Gestalt Therapy Verbatim." Lafayette, Calif.: Real People Press, 1969.

Permack, D. and Arglin, B., On the Possibilities of Self-Control in Man and Animals. "Journal of Abnormal Psychology," 1973, 81:137-151.

Rubottom, R.L., The Differences and Similarities of Zen, Autogenic Training, Hypnosis and Acupuncture. "Journal of the American Institute of Hypnosis," 1973, 14:226-227.

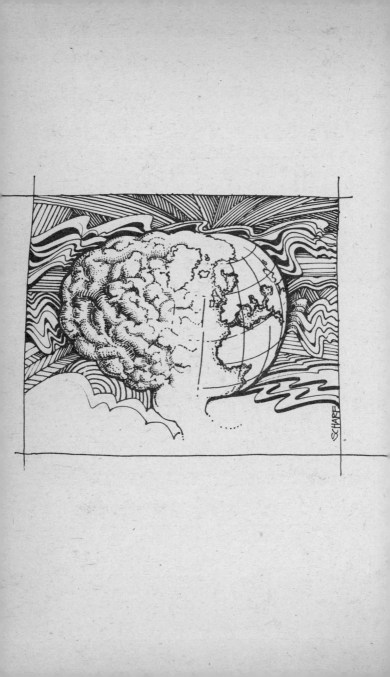

CHAPTER 3:
HOW I DISCOVERED TOTAL MIND POWER.

As a medical student at the University of Tennessee and later a resident physician at the University of California, Los Angeles, I, like many people and my medical colleagues, had heard that we use only 10 percent of our minds, which led me to wonder about the other 90 percent. Why should it be neglected? After all, if 10 percent use of our mind could do so much for us, can you imagine how much better we would function if we were able to add the other 90 percent?

Medical school is a hard grind and I wanted to know more about using my total mind. If I could use the 90 percent that lay submerged I could meet the challenges of medical school better. I wanted to tap that inner mental reservoir to increase my energy, improve my memory and at the same time, relax.

Reading volumes of materials at the medical library led me to research by Edmund Jacobson, who in the 1930s described the mental benefits of relaxation techniques.

And there were works of other notable doctors

and researchers at hand—but they were confined to medical libraries and laboratories at such respected institutions as Stanford, M.I.T. and Harvard Universities. From my studies of the subject I discovered the remarkable things the mind could influence, such as helping people maintain good health, helping the sick get better and in general providing good mental and physical stability.

With this material at hand I decided to give the information a personal test. I wanted to use more of my mind to help me through medical school in an easier fashion.

My experiences led me to relax better and I improved in my scholastic abilities. I increased my memory, I had better comprehension and concentration, and I read faster. I needed all the help I could get in medical school and through the use of more of my mind, I got it.

But my investigation into the use of the mind did not stop with graduation from medical school. It has continued through my years of practice as a doctor. I continued to probe scientific and medical journals on subjects concerned with the mind.

In my professional practice I observed that many of my patients did better if they developed a more cooperative mental attitude. At the same time there were many people who were searching for help but didn't know where to turn. Quite a few did not use their minds to influence their problems. Those who did, however, were always better able to cope with the problems of life.

What disturbed me was that help was available to everyone—the healthy who wanted to be healthier, the sick who wanted more help to overcome their ailments. But there was no practical guide for my patients to use.

Many people, I noted, sought answers to their problems from friends, various cults and beliefs and some even went as far as to sit with fortune tellers. From observations of friends I noted that those who made better use of their minds were more successful in resolving their problems while those who depended on others were less rewarded; no matter how much effort or how much they paid "outsiders."

Perhaps the most intriguing part of my research involved interviewing thousands of patients and friends to learn what their problems were and how they were handling them. In most instances I found they had very few places to turn to. Even those who offered a possibility of aid, such as physicians, psychologists, and religous counselors, could only provide partial answers.

The problems were far-ranging, from achieving career goals to enjoying better physical and emotional health. Those who succeeded were using some of the techniques of Total Mind Power—even though they were not aware they were doing so.

From all these observations and from research beginning in medical school and continuing in private practice, I developed the concepts and techniques of Total Mind Power as explained in this book.

Other doctors have learned of my techniques and are using them with their patients. This book is for those who want to learn about Total Mind Power techniques—those in the medical profession and those who do not need medical attention but want to improve themselves. Total Mind Power techniques are available to anyone willing to use his or her mind for their own benefit.

From a medical and scientific standpoint I have discovered that there are certain ways to use your mind that provide beneficial results. This book is a concise guide for showing you these ways to use your mind.

Total Mind Power can be applied to myriad problems and situations. Its use is only as limited as the user wants it to be. Its use will provide help in many of life's situations. Your mind is yours. Use all its abilities and you will be a happier, more fulfilled person with a total sense of well-being.

REFERENCES

Barber, T.X., "LSD, Marihuana, Yoga and Hypnosis." Chicago: Aldine, 1970.

Barber, T.X., "Hypnosis: A Scientific Approach." New York: Van Nostrand Reinhold Co., 1970.

Beahrs, J.O., The Hypnotic Psychotherapy of Milton H. Erickson. "American Journal of Clinical Hypnosis," 1971, 14:73-91.

Bergin, A.E. and Strupp, H.H. "Changing Frontiers in the Science of Psychotherapy." New York: Aldine-Atherton, 1972.

Cheek, D.B. and LeCron, L.M., "Clinical Hypnotherapy." New York: Grune and Stratton, 1968.

Coue, E., "The Practice of Autosuggestion." New York: Doubleday, 1922.

Erickson, M.H. and Rossi, E.L., Two Level Communication and the Microdynamics of Trance and Suggestion. "The American Journal of Clinical Hypnosis," 1976, 18:153-171.

Feinsterheim, H., "Help Without Psychoanalysis." New York: Stein and Day, 1971.

Gordon, J.E. (ed.), "Handbook of Clinical Experimental Hypnosis." New York: The Macmillan Co., 1967.

Green, A., Green, E. and Walters, D., "Psychophysiological Training for Creativity." Paper presented at the meeting of the American Psychological Association, Washington, D.C., 1971.

Kamiya, J., Autoregulation of the EEG Alpha Rhythm: A program for the Study of Consciousness. In M.H. Chase (ed.), "Operant Control of Brain Activity," 1974.

Huxley, A., "The Perennial Philosophy." New York: Harper and Row, 1970.

James, W., "The Varieties of Religious Experiences." New York: University Book, 1963.

Jung, C.G., "Modern Man in Search of a Soul." New York: Harcourt, Brace and World, Inc., 1933.

Kadushin, C., "Why People Go To Psychiatrists." New York: Aldine-Atherton, 1969.

Paul, G.L., "Insight Versus Desensitization in Psychotherapy." Stanford: Stanford University Press, 1966.

Piper, W.E. and Wagan, M., Placebo Effect in Psychotherapy: An Extension of Earlier Findings. "Journal of Consulting and Clinical Psychology," 1970, 34:447.

Maltz, M., "Psycho-Cybernetics." Englewood Cliffs: Prentice Hall, Inc., 1960.

Maslow, A.H., "Toward a Psychology of Being." New York: D. Van Nostrand Co., Inc., 1968.

Masserman, J.H. (ed.), "Current Psychiatric Therapies Vol. 13." New York: Grune and Stratton, 1973.

Mishra, R.S., "The Fundamentals of Yoga." New York: Julian Press, 1959.

Salter, A., "The Case Against Psychoanalysis." New York: Holt, Rinehart and Winston, 1952.

Stein, C., "Practical Psychotherapeutic Techniques." Springfield, Illinois: Charles C. Thomas, Publisher, 1968.

Szasz, T.S., "The Manufacture of Madness: A comparative Study of the Inquisition and the Mental Health Movement." New York: Harper and Row, Publishers, 1970.

Szasz, T.S., "Ideology and Insanity: Essays on the Psychiatric Dehumanization of Man." New York: Doubleday Anchor, 1970.

Wallace, R.K. and Benson, H., The Physiology of Meditation. "Scientific American," 1972, 226:85-90.

Walrath, L.C. and Hamilton, D.W., Autonomic Correlates of Meditation and Hypnosis. "The American Journal of Clinical Hypnosis," 1965, 17:190-197.

Weitzenhoffer, A.M., "General Techniques of Hypnotism." New York: Grune and Stratton, Inc., 1957.

Wolberg, L.R., "Medical Hypnosis Vol. 1 and 2." New York: Grune and Stratton, Inc., 1957.

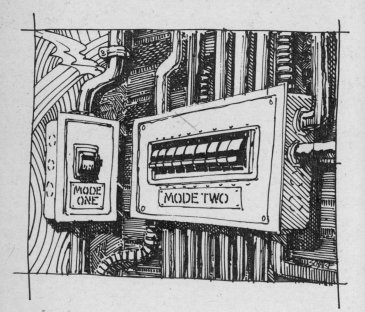

CHAPTER 4:
IF YOU ARE ALWAYS SEEKING SOLUTIONS AND
CAN'T FIND THE ANSWERS, YOU AREN'T USING
THE OTHER 90 PERCENT OF YOUR MIND.

HOW WONDERFUL IS THE MIND, YET HOW LITTLE WE
USE OF IT. In this age of electronic imagery and computerized technology we seem to have overlooked one
of our most precious assets. Somehow it is as if we
are setting our minds aside and letting the machines
take over. But, if we reflect for a few minutes, hopefully we will realize that it was the mind that created
all of this technology and not the reverse.

SOME SIMPLE FACTS ABOUT THE MIND. The largest
computer so far devised is reported to have over 100
million connections in its complicated electronic memory system. Each connection tries to duplicate electron-
ically the action of one human brain cell, the neuron.
On the other hand, each human brain has over 10 to
15 *billion* connections and neurons. So it would take
literally a thousand or more of these giant man-made
computers to equal just one human brain capacity.
And in addition to the billions of neurons the brain

has, there is a supportive system of 20 to 80 billion cells, called neuroglia cells, that back up the neurons.

THE ABILITY AND CAPACITY OF THE BRAIN CANNOT BE DUPLICATED. If we were to make just one computer to equal the capacity of one human brain, it is estimated that the computer hardware required would cover an area larger than one of our larger states, and would require so much energy to run that enough heat would be generated to warm the oceans to such a degree that it would upset the temperature balance of the world.

TEN PERCENT VERSUS NINETY PERCENT. By now you know we only use 10 percent of our minds, but you may not be sure what this means. Well, the same applies to our bodies. We only use a small amount of the physical capacity available to us. We know that basically, our bodies today have the same design they had several million years ago, but through evolution their uses have been modified. The same design that was geared toward walking great distances, perhaps climbing trees for safety from predators, hunting and other strenuous activities, is not necessary today. We sit more, use our legs less and unless you are an athlete constantly keeping your body in shape, you use less than the potential of your physical body.

Like the body, the brain has undergone evolutionary changes. The neurons discussed earlier are connected to each other by filaments, connective bridges forming a complex network. Scientists have estimated that only about 10 percent of the available neuron connections are used. More and more neurons can be brought into this great system by using the other 90 percent of your mind, thereby tapping the information processing abilities of the brain to a much greater extent.

THE BRAIN OPERATES IN TWO MODES. Through scientific research we now know that the brain operates basically on two primary levels of functioning; conscious mind functioning or the 10 percent level, and a focusing of awareness functioning or the 90 percent level. It is becoming clear that the 90 percent level is as important a mode of mental functioning as the conscious level. And it has become apparent to scientists that both levels require the use of learning procedures and techniques if they are to be used to their fullest in the advanced culture we live in.

IT BOTHERS ME BECAUSE SO MANY PEOPLE SUFFER NEEDLESSLY. With such a natural asset available—our minds—I am distressed that people do not take advantage of it to resolve their problems and provide themselves with better mental and physical health. We carry the brain with us all the time and can turn it on whenever the need requires. All we have to do is learn how to activate it and focus it on a particular problem so it can be solved.

IF YOU ARE ALWAYS SEEKING SOLUTIONS AND HAVEN'T FOUND THE ANSWERS, YOU ARE NOT USING THE OTHER 90 PERCENT OF YOUR MIND. The mind is a vast resource, it stores millions of items of information acquired over the years, integrates this material and then makes it available to us for use when the situation requires. The answers to our problems lie within ourselves, in our minds. Only the techniques for using this resource are lacking.

HOW CAN WE MASTER SUCH A COMPLEX MIND TO WORK FOR US? Although the mind is a marvelous tool, we do not have to be concerned about how it works and just be impressed with the fact that it does work for us. What has to be learned is how to cultivate the 90 percent that can help resolve our problems. That is the aim of this book.

REFERENCES

Agras, W.S., Weitenberg, H., Barlow, D.H. Curtis, N., Edwards, J. and Wright, D., Relaxation Is Systematic Desensitization. "Archives of General Psychiatry," 1971, 25:511-514.

Arnold, M.B., "Emotion and Personality, Vol. 1." New York: Columbia University Press, 1960.

Ayllon, T. and Azrin, N.H., Reinforcement and Instructions with Mental Patients. "Journal of Experimental Analysis of Behavior," 1964, 7:327.

Bandler, R. and Grinder, J., "Patterns of the Hypnotic Techniques of Milton H. Erickson, M.D., Vol. 1." Cupertino, Calif.: Meta Publications, 1975.

Bateson, G., "Steps to an Ecology of Mind." New York: Ballantine Books, 1972.

Bergin, A.E., "Handbook of Psychotherapy and Behavior Change." New York: John Wiley and Sons, 1971.

Das, J.P., "Verbal Conditioning and Behavior." Oxford, England: Pergamon Press, 1969.

DiCara, L.V., Barber, T.X., Kamiya, J., Miller, N.E., Shapiro, D. and Stovya, J. (eds.), "Biofeedback and Self-Control 1974." Chicago: Aldine Publishing Co., 1975.

Franks, C.M., "Conditioning Techniques in Clinical Practice and Research." New York: Springer, 1965.

Fromm, E. and Shor, R.E., Hypnosis: Research Developments and Perspectives." Chicago: Aldine-Atherton, 1972.

John, E.R., A Model of Consciousness. In G.E. Schwartz and D. Shapiro (eds.), "Consciousness and Self-Regulation." New York: Plenum Press, 1976, 1-50.

Kanfer, F.H. and Phillips, J.S., "Learning Foundations of Behavior Therpy." New York: Wiley, 1970.

Krasner, L., Behavior Therapy. "Annual Review of Psychology," 1971, 22:483.

Kretschner, W., Meditative Techniques in Psychotherapy. "Psychologia," 1962, 5:76-83.

Masserman, J.H., "Current Psychiatric Therapies, Vol. 12." New York: Grune and Stratton, 1972.

Melton, A.W., The Taxonomy of Human Learning: Overview. "Categories of Human Learning." New York: Academic Press, 1964.

Naranjo, C. and Ornstein, R.E., "On The Psychology of Meditation." New York: Viking Press, 1971.

Oliveau, D.C., Argras, W.S., Leitenberg, H., Moore, R.C. and Wright, D.E., Systematic Desensitization, Therapeutically Oriented Instructions and Selective Positive Reinforcement. "Behaviour Research and Therapy," 1969, 7:217.

Ornstein, R.E. (ed.), "The Nature of Human Consciousness: A Book of Readings." New York: Viking Press, 1973.

Pribram, K.H., Self-Consciousness and Intentionality. In G.E. Schwartz and D. Shapiro (eds.), "Consciousness and Self-Regulation." New York: Plenum Press, 1976, 51-100.

Straus, E., "Phenomological Psychology." New York: Basic Books, 1966.

Strickland, B., Individual Differences in Verbal Conditioning, Extinction and Awareness. "Journal of Personality, 1970, 38: 363-378.

Teyler, T.J., "Altered States of Awareness: Readings from Scientific American." San Francisco: W.H. Freeman and Co. 1972.

Thomson, R. and Sluckin, W., Cybernetics and Mental Functioning, "British Journal for the Philosophy of Science." Vol. 3, 1953.

Timmons, B. and Kamiya, J., The Psychology and Physiology of Meditation and Related Phenomena: A Bibliography. "Journal of Transpersonal Psychology," 1970, 2:41-59.

Udupa, K.N., The Scientific Basis of Yoga. "Journal of the American Medical Assoc., 1972. 220:1365.

Van Nuys, D., A Novel Technique for Studying Attention During Meditation. "Journal of Transpersonal Psychology," 1971, 2:125-133.

Wolpe, J., Learning Versus Lesions as the Basis of Neurotic Behavior. "American Journal of Psychiatry," 1956, 112:923.

Wolpe, J., "The Practice of Behavior Therapy." New York: Pergamon Press, 1973.

Wolpe, J., "Psychotherapy by Reciprocal Inhibition." Stanford: Stanford University Press, 1958.

CHAPTER 5:
TOTAL MIND POWER IS A NEW WAY OF TAPPING
YOUR ENERGY SOURCES BOTH MENTAL AND
PHYSICAL.

TOTAL MIND POWER IS A NEW WAY FOR TAPPING YOUR HIDDEN MENTAL ENERGIES. While I describe Total Mind Power as new, it has been with us since man discovered the first tool. Great men and women achieved their peaks because they used the unlimited dimensions of their minds, largely by trial and error, and explored them to their fullest. Drawing upon such potentials led them to great achievements in all areas, including history, science, mathematics, medicine, and philosophy. What is new is the distillation of this knowledge.

There has been broad research on the application of the 90 percent of the mind, but the knowledge gained from this study has remained on bookshelves and in medical and scientific journals.

An example of such research and its significance is seen in an article by Dr. Barbara B. Brown, chief of experimental physiology at the Veterans Administration Hospital, Sepulveda, California, lecturer at the UCLA Medical Center, and author of *New Mind, New Body*.

She writes: "Subconscious processes, generally interpreted as all activity of mind not recognized in conscious awareness, have been documented to possess extraordinary complexity, depth of informational resources . . . mechanisms for evaluation and judgment of integrated data, and a remarkable facility for direction and efficiency of action."

The use of Total Mind Power and its techniques have been based on the conclusions reached by such eminent scientists, researchers and scholars like Dr. Brown. Total Mind Power directs you to use that powerful, but subconscious reservoir, to bring about the results you desire.

WHAT HAS KEPT US FROM USING TOTAL MIND POWER? The focus of our culture has been socio-economic rather than oriented to individual development. As our society develops more and more into technological, science-directed industrialized states, we are trained in our schools and colleges in ways that will best serve our economically based industrial empires. We are prepared for jobs, not to be ourselves. We are educated in ways to survive in the very economic environment that created the schools in the first place. This has encouraged us to use only narrow, linear thinking.

Our society somehow has managed to squeeze out our imaginations. The intense curiosity children have, their trips of fantasy in lands of goblins and ghosts, their visions of grandeur are reduced to imagery by the portrait of life as seen on the television tube. This leads to more computerized, less imaginitive thinking as children grow up.

LACK OF KNOWLEDGE OF HOW THE MIND WORKS HELPED KEEP US FROM USING IT. It has taken centuries to learn about the mind's intricacies, its abilities, its potential. And we are still exploring what it can do for us. No wonder, then, that we have explored only the surface and learned how to use only the tip of the iceberg. But in recent years as we have become more sophisticated and knowledgeable about the ways of the mind, we have become more aware of the great potential of it that we have not yet used. This book demonstrates how to use this great potential, by ourselves, for ourselves.

THE STRESS DECADE LED US TO PILLS AND THE DRUGSTORE. As our society made rapid strides in the '40s and into the '70s (harnessing of atomic energy, man landing on the moon) and we advanced speedily into areas beyond most peoples' comprehension, stress blossomed. Rather than turning to ourselves to cope with this new era we turned to tranquilizers and pills of all sorts, and a variety of new cults and mystic religions for escape, rather than solutions. The drugstore and its contents became our crutch for support. We used our minds less and outside intervention more.

THE BREAKOUT INTO THE CONSCIOUSNESS ERA. For some, the 1960s and the 1970s became a time to probe the mind and a cultural revolution was under way. They were dissatisfied with the traditional paths of the past and were looking for new ways to identify themselves, new ways for understanding themselves, new methods for coping. The mind was the key, hopefully the link to a better understanding of life and how to survive and excel within the perimeters of this new technological society. People, mainly the young, started testing the boundaries that had been established by society. They pursued the new gurus, explored radical philosophies, absorbed mystical rituals and thinkings of the East, and involved themselves in meditation, analysis, hypnosis, and a variety of other mind-bending techniques. For some there was an awareness, but not a solution. For many, these processes provided only momentary relief. But perhaps the most beneficial aspect was the inward probing into the use of the mind for solutions.

TOTAL MIND POWER AND OTHER TECHNIQUES. While cults gather followers, they do not help people cope with the problems of society, but generally lead them away from it. The same can be said for mystic beliefs, mainly the ones that have a basis in Eastern religions. Their principles may offer some relief in the regions of the world in which they were formulated, but they are not suited to man's role in Western, industrialized societies. Meditation and chanting may offer some temporary respite, but they do not show us how to overwhelm the constant stress and strains that prevail in our society. Total Mind Power provides us with the ability to reach into ourselves to help and improve ourselves. Why do we have to turn to other sources, other supports, when the best available tool is a part of our natural being? Your mind, which absorbs so much during your lifetime and translates myriad experiences that you can draw from to meet all challenges, is a fantastic resource. It can be developed and used to its fullest, and that is what Total Mind Power shows you how to do.

TOTAL MIND POWER TECHNIQUES ARE UNIQUE. The other techniques mentioned above do not go far enough. They are like the frosting on the cake. Total Mind Power techniques penetrate beyond the surface and show us how to use that large portion of our minds—the 90 percent—that can do so much for us because it is virtually an unlimited reservoir of resources.

Total Mind Power steps are simple to follow and are based on verbal transcripts that are detailed to help you solve particular problems. These transcripts, and how to prepare and use them to meet your particular needs, will be explained in the following chapters.

Total Mind Power is a lifetime tool because it relies on something that is with you throughout life —your resourceful mind. There are countless books available on the mind, but they do not tell you what to do to harness its wonders. Consider this book as a working tool, because it takes you step-by-step to an understanding of the techniques to be used for activating your mind's total resources.

REFERENCES

Barber, T.X., DiCara, L.V., Kamiya, J., Miller, N.E., Shapiro, D. and Stoyva, J. (eds.), "Biofeedback and Self-Control 1975-76." Chicago: Aldine Publishing Co., 1976.

Barber, T.X., Responding to 'Hypnotic' Suggestions: An Introspective Report. "American Journal of Clinical Hypnosis," 1975, 18:6-22.

Beck, A.T., "Depression." New York: Harper and Row, 1967.

Breger, L. and McGaugh, J.L., Critique and Reformulation of Learning Theory Approaches to Psychotherapy and Neuroses. "Psychological Bulletin," 1965, 63:338.

Brown, B.B., Biological Awareness as a State of Consciousness. 'Journal of Altered States of Consciousness," 1975, 2:1-14.

Budzynski, T.H., Biofeedback and the Twilight States of Consciousness. In G.E. Schwartz and D. Shapiro (eds.), "Consciousness and Self-Regulation." New York: Plenum Press, 1976, 361-385.

Fagan, J. and Shepherd, I., "Gestalt Therapy Now." Palo Alto: Science and Behavior Books, 1970.

Greenough, W.T., "The Nature and Nuture of Behavior: Developmental Psychobiology: Readings from Scientific American." San Francisco: W.H. Freeman and Co., 1973.

Haley, J., "Strategies of Psychotherapy." New York: Grune and Stratton, 1963.

Lazarus, A.A., "Behavior Therapy and Beyond." New York: McGraw-Hill Book Company, 1971.

Lilly, J.C., "Programming and Meta-Programming in the Human Biocomputer." New York: The Julian Press, Inc., Publishers, 1971.

Locke, E.A., Is Behavior Therapy Behavioristic? Analysis of Wolpe's Psychotherapeutic Methods. "Psychological Bulletin," 1971, 76:318.

Meichenbaum, D., Toward a Cognitive Theory of Self-control. In G.E. Schwartz and D. Shapiro (eds.), "Consciousness and Self Regulation." New York: Plenum Press, 1976, 223-260.

Schultz, J.H. and Luthe, W., "Autogenic Training." New York: Grune and Stratton, 1959.

Skinner, B.F., "Science and Human Behavior." New York: Macmillan, 1953.

Skinner, B.F., "Beyond Freedom and Dignity." New York: Alfred A. Knopf, Inc., 1971.

Sparks, L., "Self-Hypnosis: A Conditioned Response Technique." Grune and Stratton, Inc., 1962.

Reyna, L.J., Conditioning Therapy, Learning Theories and Research. J. Wolpe, A. Salter and L.J. Reyna (eds.), "Conditioning Therapies." New York: Holt, Rinehart & Winston, 1964.

Rokeach, M., "The Open and Closed Mind." New York: Basic Books, 1960.

Woolfolk, R.L., Psychophysiological Correlates of Meditation. "Archives of General Psychiatry," 1975, 32:1326-1333.

CHAPTER 6:
DON'T WORRY ABOUT NEEDING WILL POWER
AND CONCENTRATION—THEY DON'T APPLY
TO TOTAL MIND POWER.

WITH TOTAL MIND POWER THERE IS NO STRESS, STRAIN
OR WILL POWER NECESSARY. Since Total Mind Power
encourages you to make use of a tool you already possess—90 percent of your mind—there is no strain,
concentration or will power required. You just relax
and direct the other 90 percent of your mind to
achieve your goals—effortlessly.

UNLIKE OTHER TECHNIQUES, YOU DON'T HAVE
TO UNDERSTAND WHY YOU HAVE A PROBLEM. Often
psychological consultation and other mind probing
techniques require you to understand why you have
a particular problem in order to resolve it. Total
Mind Power does not make this requirement, only
that you want to resolve the problem or want to
change a situation.

TO USE TOTAL MIND POWER EFFECTIVELY, SET
ASIDE HARD WORK AND EFFORT. Because we are
dealing with a part of our mind that has been virtually unused until now, you will have to unlearn some
of the things instilled since childhood. In learning the
techniques of Total Mind Power you can set aside some
misconceptions. Almost since childhood we have been
taught that to achieve our goals we must use will power,

concentration and sheer hard work and effort. Yet Total Mind Power works best when you do not use physical effort or strain, but rather when you let the other 90 percent of your mind do all the work.

HARD WORK BY ITSELF WON'T HELP YOU ATTAIN YOUR GOALS. In fact, all you most likely are doing is churning up a lot of steam if you are not using the creative powers of the 90 percent of your mind, which has been the driving and influential force of all significant discoveries, philosophies, and achievements. The 90 percent is the intuitive, imaginative, creative, probing and most resourceful portion of your mind. Through the use of Total Mind Power this reservoir is drawn upon and put into action.

DON'T UNDERESTIMATE TOTAL MIND POWER, BECAUSE IT IS EASY TO APPLY. While the use of Total Mind Power techniques are easy and everyone can learn them just by following the simple steps described in this book, don't underestimate what they can do. Remember, it seems simple to turn on a light bulb, but the exact way electricity works is only a theory and still not completely understood. The same can be said for Total Mind Power—the techniques appear simple, but they tap our mind's total potential whether or not we understand them completely.

WILL POWER AND CONCENTRATION ARE NOT THE BEST SOLUTION TO MOST SITUATIONS. People have been using will power and concentration for thousands of years but they still have not overcome their problems. At best, will power is only a 10 percent effort. With Total Mind Power, there is no will power involved, just a relaxing, no-stress method for putting a vast portion of your mind to work for you.

REFERENCES

Benson, H., Beary, J.F. and Carol, M.P., The Relaxation Response. "Psychiatry," 1974, 37:37-46.

Gibbons, D., "Beyond Hypnosis: Explorations in Hyperempiria." South Orange, N.J.: Power Publishing, Inc., 1973.

Goldried, M. and Goldfried, A., Cognitive Change Methods. In F. Kanfer and A. Goldstein (eds.), "Helping People Change." New York: Pergamon Press, 1975.

Goldried, M., DeCenteceo, E. and Weinberg, L., Systematic Rational Restructuring as a Self-control Technique. "Behavior Therapy." 1974, 5:247-254.

Green, E.E., Green, A.M. and Walters, E.D., Voluntary Control of Internal States: Psychological and Physiological. "Journal of Transpersonal Psychology," 1970, 2:1-26.

Kosho, U., "Approach to Zen." San Francisco: Japan Publications, 1973.

Meichenbaum, D. and Cameron, R. The Clinical Potential of Modifying What Clients Say to Themselves. "Psychotherapy: Theory, Research and Practice," 1974, 11:103-117.

Phillips, R.E., Johnson, G.D. and Geyer, A., Self-administered Systematic Desensitization. "Behaviour Research and Therapy." 1972, 10:93-96.

Platonov, K., "The Word As a Physiological and Therapeutic Factor." Moscow: Foreigh Languages Publishing House, 1959.

Reinking, R.H. and Kohl, M.L., Effects of Various Forms of Relaxation Training on Physiological and Self-report Measures of Relaxation. "Journal of Consulting and Clinical Psychology, 1975, 43:595-600.

Sheehan, P.W. (ed.) "The Function and Nature of Imagery." New York: Academic Press, 1972.

CHAPTER 7:
HOW TO DEVELOP AND USE THE POWERFUL
STEP-BY-STEP TECHNIQUES AND PROCEDURES
OF TOTAL MIND POWER FOR YOURSELF.

THREE SIMPLE STEPS COMPRISE THE BASIC TOTAL
MIND POWER TECHNIQUE. Total Mind Power techniques operate best in an environment of relaxation
without any outside disturbing interferences or stimuli. The steps are outlined in this chapter and detailed in the following ones containing transcripts
for specific problems to be resolved. Step One incorporates techniques to shut out external stimuli
such as noises, smells, harsh lighting, with a resulting *drifting of the mind into a state of focused
awareness*, which is different from your everyday
awareness. This focused state of awareness, in
which you zero in on a limited set of stimuli and not
the varied sights, sounds and sensations of everyday
living, is a different state of consciousness.

After establishing this focused state of awareness you flow into Step Two, which is *directing
your thoughts* toward your problem or the situation you want to change and visualizing or sensing

as clearly as possible, in great detail, the ideal solution you seek.

Step Three is the *sequencing* of your thoughts to bring about the desired changes. Depending on the intensity or acuteness of the problem or the situation you want changed, you schedule the use of Total Mind Power techniques on a results basis. Just as an athlete maintains his form by keeping his muscles in tone, so do the techniques of Total Mind Power work to keep you in shape, but instead of just using physical exercises, you are using mental ones. You know your problem, you determine the rapidity with which you want it resolved, using Total Mind Power.

Dr. Herbert Benson of Harvard University, author of *The Relaxation Response*, has shown clearly that even simple relaxation procedures may have profound changes on the autonomic nervous system with such effects as the reduction of high blood pressure. In his book he shows how a mental device such as gazing at objects, a passive attitude, decreased muscle tension and a quiet environment together create a bodily response that is similar to meditation.

These are similar to Step One procedures. However, they are not combined together with verbal self-directions (Total Mind Power Step Two procedure) as in the transcripts and therefore have only limited effect when compared to Total Mind Power. It should be remembered that the combination of Total Mind Power's Steps One, Two and Three is of primary importance and if any of these techniques are left out, the benefits will not be obtained.

Supportive of my conclusion that the mind can be directed specifically towards goals is research by Dr. Theodore Barber, director of psychological research at the Medfield Foundation and Medfield State Hospital, Harding, Mass., an internationally established researcher in the field of using verbal and task motivational instructions to bring about mental and physical changes.

Dr. Barber, who also has been a post-doctoral research fellow at Harvard University's Laboratory of Social Relations, in a recent scientific paper showed the possibilities of using the mind when it is directed properly in areas such as controlling pain, dreams, skin temperature, and improving nearsighted vision and controlling allergies.

The methods he describes are basically verbal. Total Mind Power's techniques are based on self-directed verbal directions. Steps One, Two and Three show you how to create these directions to make the most of your capabilities and potentials.

Remember the electric light example of the last chapter. How easy it is to flick on a light, yet how complex are the light's action and the flow of electricity. Although these techniques using the mind appear simple, and are in fact simple to do, they are powerful in their results. Complex neurophysiological changes take place in your mind and body according to the direction you give yourself in the transcripts.

USING TRANSCRIPTS AS TOTAL MIND POWER TOOLS. As indicated earlier, Total Mind Power techniques are free. The only tools needed are transcripts, which are your paths leading you into a state of focused awareness (Step One) and directing your thoughts to the ideal solution of the problem or situation you want changed (Step Two). The transcripts can be typed or written sheets you read to yourself, commit to memory, have a friend read to you, or recorded on an inexpensive tape or casette recorder and played back.

SPECIFICITY IS THE KEY TO TOTAL MIND POWER'S SUCCESS. Because you know your situation best, your own self-directed transcripts will help you resolve it the best way possible. You and your mind are the vital factors in overcoming a particular problem and in the specific manner you want it resolved. You are not bothered by outside consultation or interference that can only offer partial answers to your needs.

THE THREE STEPS

The following pages are devoted to a detailed explanation of the three simple but powerful steps of Total Mind Power.

STEP ONE: A FOCUSING OF AWARENESS. Daily we are subjected to a variety of stimuli to our senses of taste, touch, sight, smell, and hearing. Everything around us provokes our senses—food, weather, clothing, people, lights, signs, noises, eating. Many of these stimuli are irritating and are unconsciously screened out or life would be chaotic. Our ability to detour the irritating stimuli makes life bearable.

However, most people are coping with more sensations than they need and can handle. When you use Total Mind Power techniques to cut out more of the bombarding sensations that are competing for your attention, most of which are nonessential, your mind can focus its awareness on the area to which you are directing it. No longer overloaded with unnecessary stimuli, your mind is able to concentrate all its power on achieving your chosen goal.

Step One of the Total Mind Power techniques helps cancel out most of the nonessential sensations.

To help achieve the level of focused awareness, the environment should be one where comfort and no outside distractions reign. Select a place neither too hot or too cold, close your eyes, cutting out visual sensations as well as others—aromas, noises—that will detour you from focusing on your desired subject.

Choose the time of day you believe most suitable for Step One focusing of awareness. Evening, before going to sleep, or just after awakening are times suggested. But the important thing is you alone determine what time is best for you.

Some hints to help you desensitize yourself to outside stimuli include locating a television channel that is not broadcasting and turning up the volume. The rushing sounds that result can be a highly effective screen against outside noise. Other barriers to troublesome noises can be ear plugs, melodious music and even monotonous beats. Visual interferences can be blocked out by cutting a ping-pong ball in half and placing each half over an eye. Also, weak strobe lights that provide a rhythm of 12 beats per second —coinciding approximately with the rhythm of your alpha brain waves—will screen out visual sensations. People with a history of epilepsy or those uncomfortable with strobe lights should avoid this method.

However, none of these mechanical techniques are really necessary, for simply relaxing and closing your eyes in a quiet room is very effective. And after some experience you'll be able achieve a focusing of awareness even in very hectic situations.

Above all, a relaxing state of mind and body is emphasized. Total Mind Power techniques can be used in any comfortable sitting or lying position. The aim is to set up an ideal situation in which the mind can drift on its own, without effort, concentration or fatigue, into a focused awarness in the direction you set.

STEP TWO: DIRECTING YOUR MIND. When you have moved through Step One and your mind has reached a focusing of awareness, you are ready to deal with the specific situation or problem and to direct your thoughts to correct unsatisfactory areas of your life or to move toward the goal you have selected.

In Step Two you apply the techniques to draw from your reservoir of experiences and information to attain a solution for your specific situation or problem, to change your entire life for the better. Your mind will work effectively for you only when *self-directed* in a manner that is suitable only for you. Meditation alone, for example, often fails because it does not direct the mind to a specific area, especially when concerned with problems of health. In Step Two you focus in on your specific area of concern and you come up with the best possible solution, which is incorporated into your Step Two transcript. During this step every possible sense and appropriate emotion must be used to get the job done. The more imaginative you are in preparing your transcript, the more success you will have. The sample Step Two transcripts in Chapters 9 through 30 give examples of vivid directions you can use for many typical problems and situations. I suggest that you read through them completely even if they do not apply to one of your own problems. By so doing you will get a much clearer idea of how transcripts are structured. Go through them and list how many sensations and emotions are called upon, and notice the similar pattern in their construction.

STEP THREE: SEQUENCING YOUR MIND DIRECTIONS. The essence of this step is the proper repetition of the first two steps. The frequency can only be determined by the results you obtain. There are no controlled studies or statistical research to show what frequency produces the most satisfactory results. Also the problem with which you are concerned has a bearing on how often you make use of the techniques.

For example, if you are applying Total Mind Power to relieve tension, you might want to use the techniques only when you face certain stressful and tense situations. But if you suffer long-standing anxiety, you might need to apply the techniques daily until the stress is under control.

If weight control is your goal and you already have achieved some success through the use of Total Mind Power techniques, you may need to apply them only once a week or once a month. In some situations, once the problem has been controlled, Total Mind Power techniques may never need to be used again for the particular problem. The emphasis should be on applying Total Mind Power techniques until the results you want are achieved, and then using them only as necessary to maintain your results.

My own experience with Total Mind Power techniques, plus an analysis of the medical literature suggests that for most situations transcripts be used daily for one week to start, then every other day for the second week, then once a week for the third week, and then as needed to maintain results.

TOTAL MIND POWER MAY BE APPLIED TO ALL OF YOUR PROBLEMS, AND MAY BE EFFECTIVE FOR MORE THAN ONE PROBLEM AT A TIME. For example, relaxing your mind and body may relieve the symptoms of a migraine headache, even if a specific transcript was not prepared for headache relief. And you may make transcripts for, and work on as many problems as you choose at any one time.

PREPARING YOUR TRANSCRIPTS

The essence of using Total Mind Power is the transcript. It is the written prescription for better health, better mental attitude and a better life. And it requires no doctor to prescribe it, no pills or medication to use, only the use of your mind and its application to the problem you have or the situation you want changed.

WHAT IS A TRANSCRIPT? It is your training paper —simple directions to yourself to aid in focusing your mind on the problem and the resolving of it. Transcripts contained in this book—and they are a major portion of it—have been prepared to aid you in resolving a number of problems I have seen disturbing many of my patients. They can be used as offered, altered to fit your particular need, or just used as examples or models from which you can prepare your own. The importance of Total Mind Power techniques is that it is you who draws up a transcript that you believe will offer the best solution to the situation in which you are involved, which you want to improve.

TRANSCRIPTS CAN BE TYPED OR WRITTEN PAGES THAT YOU READ TO YOURSELF, MEMORIZE, HAVE SOMEONE READ TO YOU, OR RECORDED, WHICHEVER SEEMS TO BE THE MOST PRACTICAL MANNER. The playback of a recording provides you with your own directions in your own voice and you can carry it with you so you can put Total Mind Power to use whenever the need arises.

Also, with a recording you can relax, close your eyes and eliminate distractions. And effectiveness is enhanced because no one else is in the relaxed environment but you, whereas if someone is reading the transcript to you there may be a sense of self-consciousness and lack of privacy. Even when there are other people around, the use of headphones or earphones will enable you to keep your transcript playback private.

LENGTH OF TRANSCRIPTS. For Step One, focusing your awareness, the transcript should be about 10 minutes long, while for Step Two, in which you provide yourself directions about your problem or situation, the length should be about 20 minutes. You may find as you prepare your transcripts that they can be shortened to as little as 15 minutes in all, but they do not need to exceed 45 minutes.

Pause during the making of your recording, so that when you listen to it you will have ample time to follow the directions. Also during the recording of your transcript, put yourself into a relaxed mood, for this will be reflected in your voice and will provide a pleasant playback.

A KEY TO THE SUCCESS OF TOTAL MIND POWER IS NOT CONCENTRATION OR ENFORCED WILL POWER. Rather, it is a gentle ride into a focused awareness, which is the basis for your self directions to be effective. Without focusing your awareness you would be directing only about 10 percent of your mind. Once your awareness is focused, your directions are reaching the other 90 percent of your mind and *you will be using the other 90 percent of your mind*.

STEP ONE TRANSCRIPT: EXAMPLE NO. 1. The following transcript, and all the transcripts in this book, have been carefully prepared to cover all the principles as outlined in this chapter. They have been analyzed to make sure they cover all the points of directing your mind, taking into account the proper order and time sequences of the directions.

You may want to alter these to suit your individual needs, or to prepare new ones of your own. These transcripts provide a practical, carefully thought out framework within which you can develop your own. However, they can be recorded or copied directly from the book for your personal use, so that you can start immediately to improve and change your life.

Here is an example of a transcript you may use for Step One of Total Mind Power, which will lead you to a focusing of your awareness:

Make yourself very comfortable and relaxed.

Close your eyes and imagine in your mind's eye a beautiful,
helium-filled balloon.

You see yourself very,
very comfortable in the basket of the balloon as it
is about to be launched from a large,
open field.

You feel comfortable and very confident about the journey you are about to take,
and you have great expectations of happiness as the balloon lifts gently off the field.

You see the balloon lifting into the air,
and it's a bright,
warm,
sunny summer afternoon.

The balloon shimmers in the sunlight with a deep, blue-green color.

As the balloon lifts up higher and higher,
you find yourself more and more relaxed,
and your mind expands into an overwhelming feeling
of joy and exhilaration.

You become very interested in all of the sights
around you,
and you can hear the gentle floating of the balloon
through the air.

You are not familiar with the landscape that
the balloon is drifting over,
but you take great interest in it because of its beauty.

There isn't a cloud in the sky.

You can see a full moon coming up over the
horizon,
even though it's still afternoon.

The balloon drifts very slowly,
very comfortably across open meadows and fields,
passing over rivers and streams,
and you can breathe the freshness of the air that
surrounds you.

With each breath you take,
you find yourself feeling more and more exhilarated.

You are now passing over a new-mown field
of wheat,
and the smell of the fresh-cut wheat fills your nostrils

and brings back memories of your childhood,
when you walked through freshly-cut grass.

All of the colors of the wheat field play upon
your mind as the sun shimmers in glistening patterns
on the uncut,
waving wheat.

You can hear the sound of a threshing machine
as it makes a path through the fields.

Your balloon drifts past these fields and starts
floating over a beautiful,
deep blue lake.

A cool sensation is felt over your skin as you
drift farther and farther across the lake,
and it's a very inspiring sight.

You can also see the reflection of the moon as
it rises higher in the afternoon sky,
next to the reflection of the drifting balloon.

It's one of the most beautiful pictures you can
ever remember seeing.

As the afternoon progresses, your balloon
continues to drift.

A few stars can be seen in the blue sky as dusk
approaches.

The sky is filled with the beautiful light of the
full moon,

and other stars begin to appear as the sun starts to
sink over the horizon.

You watch the sun very closely as it approaches
the horizon,
and it appears as a perfect golden disk.

As the sun approaches the horizon,
the speed with which it approaches seems to increase,
and it sinks below the horizon.

A sunset now appears.

It has some of the most beautiful colors and
patterns you have ever seen.

The sunset appears to be a beautiful collage of
shapes and colors that fills you with awe of the universe.

All of your anxieties and tensions seem to float
away over the horizon as you stare in wonder at
the sunset.

It fades slowly.

The moon is lifting higher in the sky as you
float along in your beautiful,
magical balloon.

Now the stars become very clear and seem to
have a dazzling brightness that intrigues you.

Different stars have different color patterns as
they flicker with a rhythm that gives universal
movement to the entire night sky.

You feel a complete oneness with the entire
universe as you drift along,

taking in all of the colors and rhythms.

You feel in harmony with all of creation,
and it's as if your entire life is centered around this
moment.

A very peaceful sensation of fulfillment flows
through your body,
and you feel attainment of a perfect peace.

Now the night sky is starting to fade,
and beautiful patterns of light appear over the horizon
where the sun is about to rise.

Your balloon is now drifting over a beautiful
green forest as the sun begins to rise in the sky.

You can see brightly colored birds in the trees,
and you hear their sounds very clearly.

A new day is beginning for you,
and your balloon drifts back to the field where you
started.

Your mind recalls all of the beautiful moments
of your journey as your balloon settles to an easy
landing in the soft field.

You get out of the balloon's basket and lie down
in the soft grass.

You wonder at the marvels of the world.

You become more and more relaxed with each
breath you take,
and you remain very peaceful and contented.

An alternate transcript for Step One is a technique involving color.

Close your eyes, then look up toward your forehead. Pinpoints of color are superimposed against the darkness.

When doing this, you should be as comfortable as possible, as in the other Step One methods. This technique also lends itself well to the time just before you fall asleep. After you have completed the session, you can drift into a deep, peaceful sleep. Your mind will work for you powerfully throughout the night.

Increasing The Benefits of Total Mind Power While You Sleep and Dream, a later chapter, further explores this phenomenon.

Here is the "color" transcript which also includes a transition to Step Two of Total Mind Power:

Close your eyes and look toward the inner part of your mind,

behind your forehead or eyelids.

There you will notice small fragments of color.

These colors seem to change and form unusual patterns.

At first,

as you begin to relax,

they may start out as yellow,

red or orange bits of color.

As you become more relaxed,

you notice that the colors begin to become blue, green and deep blue-green.

The more you relax,

the clearer the colors become.

They may seem to pulsate in a rhythm that
relaxes you more and more.

You may squeeze your eyelids tightly together now,
then relax them.

When you squeeze them together,
you notice the colors seem to change and form even
more intriguing patterns.

After you have relaxed your eyelids,
you notice that you become even more at ease and very,
very comfortable.

The particles of blue and green colors tend to
become larger and larger.

They move in and out in a circular pattern,
and you focus your awareness upon the colors as you
become more and more relaxed.

Now,
with each breath you take,
you notice that the colors change with the rhythm
of your breathing.

With each deep breath you take,
the colors become a deep blue-green,
and when you exhale,
they become lighter blue and green.

The patterns of the colors continue to shift

back and forth,
and you feel a sense of lightness.

All the day's tensions and anxieties seem to flow from your body as if they are being drawn off into the air,
just to float away.

With each breath you take,
the patterns become more and more complicated.

You become enraptured with the colors,
and all other sounds,
movements and lights around you seem to focus the colors more strongly in your mind.

You pay less and less attention to these outside stimulations.

You begin to drift into a beautiful daydream,
and nothing seems to disturb you.

You are completely relaxed,
and nearly ready to direct your mind to Step Two of Total Mind Power.

You continue to focus the colors in your mind.

You now think about the different muscles of your body,
and you direct your attention to the ones that are most tense and tight.

You direct your attention to one muscle that

you have chosen,
perhaps a scalp muscle or a thigh muscle.

You visualize in your mind a color around that
muscle.

A tense muscle usually would have a yellow or
red aura around it.

As you watch the color around this muscle,
you direct your mind to relax it,
and relieve this tension.

As the muscle relaxes,
the color changes from yellow,
red or orange into a blue or green color,
and when the muscle is completely relaxed,
it developes a deep blue-green color around it.

Now you let your entire body relax even more,
and you bathe your entire body in a deep blue-green
color.

You can see in your mind the same deep blue-
green color forming relaxing,
rhythmic patterns.

This relaxation will stay with you throughout
Step Two of Total Mind Power,
which you will continue in just a few moments.

The preceding transcripts may be read to you by yourself or someone else, recorded directly, and may be modified as you wish to meet your particular needs. The important thing is to be relaxed, to avoid stress, and to follow your own inclination.

The focusing of awareness achieved by Step One is increased and expanded by Step Two, and some of the techniques employed interchange. After you have proceeded once through the steps as outlined, you may find that you can proceed very rapidly through Step One and be quickly ready for Step Two.

WITH STEP TWO YOU PROCEED FROM FOCUSED AWARENESS TO DIRECTING YOUR MIND TO DEAL WITH SPECIFIC PROBLEMS OR TO MOVING TOWARD ACHIEVEMENT OF A HIGHER GOAL. Your transcript should be prepared so it will direct your mind to do for you what you want it to do, whether it be for overcoming an illness or improving your backstroke on the tennis court.

Transcripts that can be used for specific situations are outlined in the following pages. Again, they can be used as they are or altered for your specific needs. Also, you can draw up your own transcripts. The ones here are a cross-section of common problems. The situation in which you are involved or bothered by may not be illustrated in this book, but these can be used as examples of how you can prepare your own directions to best fit your needs.

It's important to keep in mind and to be aware that the directions given in Step One for focusing your awareness may overlap and blend with some of the directions you give yourself in Step Two. Also, the two steps augment each other, and some directions in Step Two may even increase your focusing of awareness.

DEPENDING ON YOUR NEED, THE TRANSCRIPTS USED IN STEP ONE AND TWO ARE YOUR TOOLS FOR STEP THREE. In the third step you determine the frequency or repetition of their use. Because it is your mind, which has reactions or responsiveness different from anyone else's, schedule the use of transcripts by the results you obtain. The basic idea is that you are the master of the use of Total Mind Power. The transcripts and your mind are always available. Apply them in accordance with *your* needs.

Focus your awareness in Step One, direct your mind in Step Two and reinforce the directions as needed in Step Three. With this combination you will better control your life without being unduly influenced by all the pressures of your environment or by a society that claims to know what is best for everyone, but not necessarily you.

A thorough reading of this book and the application of techniques illustrated will assure you a healthier and more meaningful life, and above all, one in which you map out the directions you want to follow.

REFERENCES

Barber, T.X., Physiological Effects of Hypnosis and Suggestion. "Biofeedback and Self-Control 1970." Chicago: Aldine-Atherton, 1971, 188-256.

Barber, T.X., Suggested Hypnotic Behavior: The Trance Paradigm Versus an Alternative Paradigm. E.Fromm and R.E. Shor (eds.), "Hypnosis: Research Developments and Perspectives." Chicago: Aldine-Atherton Publishers, 1972, 114-182.

Bem, S., Verbal Self-control: The Establishment of Effective Self-Instruction. "Journal of Experimental Psychology," 1967, 74:485-491.

Benson, H., "The Relaxation Response." New York: William Morrow and Company, Inc, 1975.

Budzynski, T.H., Some Applications of Biofeedback Produced Twilight States. "Biofeedback and Self-Control 1972," 1973, 145-151.

Cartwright, R.D., The Influence of a Conscious Wish on Dreams: A Methodological Study of Dream Meaning and Function. "Journal of Abnormal Psychology," 1974, 83:387-393.

Cohen, D.B., Toward a Theory of Dream Recall. "Psychological Bulletin," 1974 81:138-154.

Cory, T.L., Prediting the Frequency of Dream Recall. "Journal of Abnormal Psychology," 1975, 84:261-266.

Davison, G., Tsujimoto, R. and Glaros, A., Attribution and the Maintenance of Behavior Change in Falling Asleep. "Journal of Abnormal Psychology," 1973, 82:124-133.

Dement, W., et al, "Sleep and Altered States of Consciousness." Baltimore: Williams & Wilkins, 1967.

DeSoille, R., "The Directed Daydream, A Monograph." New York: The Psychosynthesis Research Foundation, 1965.

Foulkes, D., Dream Reports From Different Stages of Sleep. "Journal of Abnormal and Social Psychology," 1962, 65:14-25.

Foulkes, D. and Vogel, G., Mental Activity at Sleep Onset. "Journal of Abnormal Psychology," 1965, 70:231-243.

French, A.P., Therapeutic Application of a Simple Relaxation Method. "American Journal of Psychotherapy." 1974, 28: 282-287.

Green, E.E., Walters, D.E., Green, A.M. and Murphy, G., Feedback Technique for Deep Relaxation. "Psychophysiology," 1969, 6:371-377.

Hammer, M., The Directed Daydream Technique. "Psychotherapy: Theory, Research and Practice," 1967, 4:173-181.

Hart, J.T., Autocontrol of EEG Alpha. "Psychophysiology," 1968, 4:506.

Heron, W., Cognitive and Physiological Effects of Perceptual Isolation. In P. Solomon, P. Kubzansky, P. Leiderman, J. Leiderman, J. Mendelson, R. Trumbull and D. Wexler (eds.), "Sensory Deprivation." Cambridge, Mass.: Harvard University Press, 1966.

Hilgard, E.R. and Nowlis, D.P., The Contents of Hypnotic Dreams and Night Dreams: An Exercise in Methodology. In E. Fromm and R.E. Shor (eds.). "Hypnosis: Research Developments and Perspectives." Chicago: Aldine-Atherton, 1972, 85-113.

Horowitz, M.J., "Image Formation and Cognition." New York: Appleton-Century-Crofts, 1970.

Jacobson, E., "Progressive Relaxation." Chicago: University of Chicago Press, 1938.

Katz, D., Relaxation Due to Verbal Suggestion: A Psychophysiological Study. "The Psychological Record," 1974, 24:523-532.

Kleitman, N., "Sleep and Wakefulness." Chicago: The University of Chicago Press, 1963.

Klinger, E., "Structure and Functions of Fantasy." New York: McGraw Hill Publishers, 1971.

Koulack, D., Rapid Eye Movements and Visual Imagery During Sleep. "Psychological Bulletin." 1972, 78:155-157.

Leuner, H., Guided Effective Imagery. "American Journal of Psychotherapy," 1969, 23:4-21.

Luthe, W., "Autogenic Therapy." New York: Grune and Stratton, 1969.

Masters, R.E.I. and Houston, J, "The Varieties of Psychedelic Experiences." New York: Holt Reinhart, 1966.

Masters, R. and Houston, J., "Mind Games." New York: Dell Publishing Co., 1972.

Mather, M.D., A Comparative Study of Hypnosis and Relaxation. "British Journal of Medical Psychology," 1975 48:55-63.

Nourse, J.C. and Welch, R.B., Emotional Attributes of Color: A Comparison of Violet and Green. "Perceptive Motor Skills," 1971, 32:403-406.

Nowlis, D.P. and Kamiya, J., The Control of Electroencephalographic Alpha Rhythms Through Auditory Feedback and the Associated Mental Activity. "Psychophysiology," 1970, 6: 476-484.

Paul, G.L., Physiological Effects of Relaxation Training and Hypnotic Suggestion. "Journal of Abnormal Psychology," 1969, 74:425.

Phillips, L.W., Training of Sensory and Imaginal Responses in Behavior Therapy. In R.D. Rubin, H. Fensterheim, A.A. Lazarus and C.M. Franks (eds.). "Advances in Behavior Therapy." New York: Academic Press, 1971.

Redfering, D.L., Influences of Differential Instructions on the Frequency of Dream Recall. "Journal of Clinical Psychology," 1974, 30:268-271.

Rossi, E.L., Self Reflection in Dreams. "Psychotherapy: Theory, Research, Practice," 1972, 290-298.

Rubin, F., Learning and Sleep. "Nature," 1970, 226-477.

Sacerdote, P, "Induced Dreams." New York: Vintage Press, 1967.

Samuels, M. and Samuels, N., "Seeing with the Mind's Eye." New York: Random House-Bookworks, 1975.

Sarte, J.P., "The Psychology of Imagination." New York: Washington Square Press, 1966.

Sarbin, T.R. and Juhasz, J.B., Toward a Theory of Imagination. "Journal of Personality," 1970, 38:52-76.

Segal, S.J., "The Adaptive Functions of Imagery." New York: Academic Press, 1971.

Segal, S.J. (ed.), "Imagery: Current Cognitive Approaches." New York: Academic Press, 1971.

Sheehan, P. (ed.), "The Function and Nature of Imagery." New York: Academic Press, 1972.

Singer, J., "Daydreaming." New York: Random House 1966.

Spanos, N.P., Valois, R., Ham, M.W. and Ham, M.L., Suggestibility and Vividness and Control of Imagery. "International Journal of Clinical and Experimental Hypnosis," 1973, 21:305-311.

Spanos, N.P., Ham, M.W. and Barber, T.X., Suggested Visual Hallucinations: Experimental and Phenomenological Data. "Journal of Abnormal Psychology," 1973, 81: 96-106.

Starker, S., Daydreaming Styles and Nocturnal Dreaming. "Journal of Abnormal Psychology," 1974, 83:52-55.

Tart, C.T., Toward the Experimental Control of Dreaming: A review of the Literature. "Psychological Bulletin," 1965, 64:81-91.

Vogel, G., Foulkes, D. and Trosman, H., Ego Functions and Dreaming During Sleep Onset. "Archives of General Psychiatry," 1966, 14:238-248.

Walker, P.C. and Johnson, R.F.Q., The Influence of Presleep Suggestions on Dream Content: Evidence and Methodological Problems. "Psychological Bulletin," 1974, 81:362-370.

Wallace, R.K. and Benson, H., The Physiology of Meditation. "Scientific American," 1972, 226:84-90.

Wallace, R.K., Benson, H. and Wilson, A.F., A Wakeful Hypometabolic Physiologic State. "American Journal of Physiology, 1971, 221:795-799.

Walpert, E.A. and Trosman, H., Studies in Psychophysiology of Dreams. I.Experimental Evocation of Sequential Dream Episodes. "Archives of Neurology and Psychiatry," 1958, 79:603-606.

Yorkston, N.J. and Sergeant, H.G.S., Simple Method of Relaxation. "Lancet," 1962, 2:1319-1321.

CHAPTER 8:
WHAT TO EXPECT AND HOW TO KNOW YOU'RE
GETTING RESULTS FROM APPLYING TOTAL
MIND POWER.

The use of Total Mind Power, I believe, is the most
powerful and positive method for the resolution of
your problems and overall improvement of yourself.
Don't be concerned whether or not Total Mind Power
techniques are working for you, because they are as
long as you follow the step-by-step techniques, and
you can later prove they are working by the results
you get.

HOW DO YOU DETERMINE IF YOU ARE IN THE
STATE OF FOCUSED AWARENESS? Your feelings will
be different. You may feel as if you are floating in
a bath of clouds, you may feel effervescent, sparkling,
or you may have specific sensory experiences. For example, if you believe you are walking through a garden
of roses you may "smell" their distinctive aromas, even
though your senses are not stimulated by the scent of
a real flower. Remember, the intensity of your imag-

ination when you are focusing your awareness will be
reflected in the variety of reactions you receive during
this state. Other things you may notice while you are
in the level of focused awareness are feelings of motion,
floating, or swirling—yet you are not actually engaged
in any of these actions, but are reclining or sitting in
a comfortable, relaxed position.

YOUR SITUATION, EXPECTATIONS, AND LIFE'S
CIRCUMSTANCES HAVE BEEN STORED IN THAT VAST
RESERVOIR, THAT 90 PERCENT OF YOUR MIND. They
all help flavor the feelings and stirrings you have while
you are in the state of focused awareness. Remember
it is *your* mind that will determine how you respond
to the stimuli, and you will be reacting to your own
experiences and expectations. The feelings people using Total Mind Power get are as varied as their personalities. Each of us is an individual, and we vary in
our reactions even to the same stimuli. So if you know
someone who also is using Total Mind Power, do not
necessarily expect the same feelings and experiences
he or she has.

OTHER CHANGES YOU WILL SEE WILL BE CHANGES
IN YOUR PROBLEM OR SITUATION. Depending, of course,
on the intensity of it, you will find what is troubling
you diminishing gradually as you continue to apply
Total Mind Power completely. Such annoyances as
headaches and other psychosomatic pains will fade and
no longer bother you. If you are seeking an improvement in your tennis game, as you apply that 90 percent
of your mind you will see positive changes on the courts.
If you are overweight and applying Total Mind Power
techniques to lose weight, you will find your solution
to the problem as the excess pounds are lost.

YOU WILL KNOW THE RESULTS BY YOUR ACCOM-
PLISHMENTS. As you become more familiar with the
techniques of Total Mind Power and use them with
greater ease, you will see the results. Whether you
think you are focusing your mind or not does not matter because you will be to some degree. . .just by following the three steps. You may not think you are
using Total Mind Power, but if you are following the
procedures in this book, listening to your transcripts,
then Total Mind Power is working for you. The degree
of its effectiveness is determined by your results. The
results may be gradual at first, but continued application
will make them complete, and occasional application
over time will maintain your results.

KEEP A RECORD OF THE RESULTS. As you use
Total Mind Power maintain a record of your program
and your progress. Use the form provided in the back
of the book, or one similar to it. Each time you use
Total Mind Power, chart the results so you can see how
you are reaching your goal. Each time you chart your
progress you will be reinforcing your faith in Total Mind
Power and it will work wonders for you. The results
and benefits you get are the best indications that Total
Mind Power is working for you to solve your problems
and improve your well-being. You will see you are strug-
gling less with your problems and starting to use more
of your mind.

WHILE YOU USE TOTAL MIND POWER FOR A SPECIFIC
PROBLEM OR SITUATION, YOU WILL FIND OTHER IMPROVE-
MENTS. While you direct your mind to resolve a partic-
ular problem you will find other beneficial side effects.
When Total Mind Power is applied to a specific problem
or situation it tends not only to resolve the particular

disturbance, but also provides a bonus—such as overall feelings of improved health and well-being. For as you conquer one problem your other bodily and mental functions are revitalized and rejuvenated.

Biochemical and metabolic functions are thought to be linked to mental performance. Therefore, when one is improved, improvements in other areas should follow. Enhanced feelings of well-being also contribute to sharper mental performance.

REFERENCES

Barber, T.X. and Ham, M.V. "Hypnotic Phsnomenon." Morristown: General Learning Press, 1974.

Jourard, S., "Explorations in Human Potential." Springfield, Ill.: Charles C. Thomas Publishing, 1966.

Jung, C.G., "Memories, Dreams, Reflections." New York: Vintage Books, 1963.

Martin, I.C., Promotion Differential Relaxation. "Journal of the Royal College of General Practitioners," 1973, 23:485-494.

Merlean-Ponty, M., "The Phenomenology of Perception." London: Routledge and Degan Paul, 1962.

Metzner, R., "Maps of Consciousness." New York: Collier, 1971.

Richardson, A., "Mental Imagery." New York: Springer Publishing Co., 1969.

Sarbin, T.R., On the Recently Reported Psysiological and Pharmacological Reality of the Hypnotic State. "Psychological Record." 1973, 23:505-511.

Tart, C.T., "Altered States of Consciousness." New York: John Wiley and Sons, Inc., 1969.

Wenger, M.A. and Bagchi, B.K., Studies of Autonomic Functions in Practitioners of Yoga in India. "Behavioral Science," 1961, 6:312-323.

PROLOGUE TO TRANSCRIPTS

Note: All the experiences related in the following chapters are true. They are the experiences of friends or patients who have consulted with me and turned to using Total Mind Power where I believed a solution could be found to their problems or to improve their situations. The names are changed, of course.

CHAPTER 9:
INCREASING THE BENEFITS OF TOTAL MIND
POWER WHILE YOU SLEEP AND DREAM.

Interest in the mystery of sleep and dreams has existed since the beginning of recorded history. The ancient Greeks erected dream temples for the regeneration of the mind and for healing purposes.

Sigmund Freud produced entire manuscripts dealing with this intriguing subject. Today, extensive medical and scientific study is devoted to dreaming and its implications for the individual. Yet with all this, there are few areas so shrouded in mystery.

Priscilla Walker and R.F.Q. Johnson of the Medfield Foundation, Medfield, Mass., in a research article state that both experimental and clinical data "have indicated that with some subjects the administration of pre-sleep suggestions to dream on a specific topic can influence the content of nocturnal dreams."

Total Mind Power techniques can be employed to increase the effects of pre-sleep directions in your dreams. And as indicated in this chapter, the ability to direct your dreams can have beneficial results.

The average person spends about one third of his

life sleeping. Most of this time is wasted as far as using the mind for specific benefit is concerned, although in general it serves to regenerate the mind and body. Some schools of psychology believe that "normal" dreaming affects our mental health, and that derangement of the pattern may result in emotional disturbance. This theory gained credence when it was discovered that when dreams were deliberately interrupted, emotional imbalances occurred.

Even though you do not dream continuously during sleep, it is believed that the mind functions at high levels during this period. These hours can be used to maximum advantage through Total Mind Power.

The mind can be directed to work for you during sleep with the same strength as in wakefulness, but with added advantages. It is used in an effortless manner, and sleep provides a ready-made screen against stimulations.

Among the major benefits to be gained from using Total Mind Power during sleep are the ability to recall dreams when you arise in the morning, the power to control your dreams, to program what you wish to dream about, and the power to turn your mind power in the direction of overcoming difficulties or solving difficult problems. All this can be accomplished without interfering with the recharging of your bodily systems, which is one of sleep's purposes.

Dreams can be pleasant experiences, and if carried over into our conscious memory can provide us with rewarding feelings. A doctor I know, Stan, discussed the functions of the mind with me and some colleagues at a dinner and the subject of dreaming came up.

Stan, a cheerful, outgoing type, said he had beautiful and wonderful dreams but could recall only a few of them when he awakened. Obviously some of his dreams were so delightful that he felt deprived of their comfort when he couldn't remember them.

"Wouldn't it be wonderful if we could recall our dreams and also select the things we would like to dream about?" Stan said. He was amazed when I told him that scientific studies showed that such a recollection and selection is possible. Here was a man of acknowledged medical skills who knew how to apply them well in the everyday art of healing the body, but when it came to research of the mind he was unaware of the great possibilities it offered.

When I described how Total Mind Power could enhance the beauty of his dreams, Stan listened attentively and agreed to apply Total Mind Power techniques. Some time later he said he was having the most beautiful dreams he ever had and was able to remember them clearly when he awoke. He was able to be selective about the things he wanted to dream about, and all of this gave him tremendous pleasures and a brighter outlook each day.

Also, directing the things he wanted to dream about had beneficial side affects in his medical profession. Stan said when he had certain difficult medical problems he would direct his mind to solve them before he went to sleep, and quite often when he awoke they would be resolved.

So for Stan, discovering the use of Total Mind Power provided him not only with a healthier frame of mind but also with an aid he could use in his medical profession to help his patients.

The following Step Two transcript can be used just before you go to sleep to direct your mind to remember your dreams. Like all Step Two transcripts, it should be used following the Step One transcript for focusing awareness:

You see yourself arising in the morning,
immediately after having a very wonderful and
beautiful dream.

You have a note pad and pencil, or a tape
recorder next to your bed,
and you immediately record the contents of your dream.

You see that you have developed a very keen
sense of awareness about your dreams,
and an interest in trying to remember them.

You hear yourself saying that you will make
an attempt to remember,
upon awakening,
all of your beautiful dreams each time they occur.

Before you go to sleep you imagine yourself
thinking about the dream you would like to have.

You feel yourself creating this dream in your
mind with all of your imagination,
and it gives you a tremendous sense of pleasure
and satisfaction to know that you will have a
beautiful dream.

You picture yourself visualizing the dream that
you would like to dream.

You see yourself applying the techniques of
Total Mind Power to direct your mind to remember
your dreams.

Now you hear yourself describing the dream
that you would like to have,
over and over again.

In a few short moments that dream runs through
your mind a thousand times.

You can *feel* the dream . . . you can *see* the
dream . . . you can *hear* the dream . . . you can *taste*
the dream . . . and you can *smell* the dream.

Now you imagine yourself reading or listening
to the record you made of the dream,
and you remember every single detail.

Your mind goes back to the dream and it pleases
you tremendously.

Since you know that you have a diary of your
dream that you can refer to at any time to refresh
your memory,
you feel complete confidence about enjoying your
dream.

The second facet of using Total Mind Power in
connection with dreams is to control the subject matter. You can have not only the ability to recall your
dreams in minute detail, but also to create the dreams
you desire.

This sample transcript shows how you can direct
your mind to work for you while you sleep:

You visualize yourself lying in bed before you go
to sleep,
and you see yourself going through Step One,
the focusing of awareness.

You feel yourself very relaxed and comfortable.

Now you imagine yourself directing your mind
toward the problem that you would like to solve,
and you hear yourself repeating the directions over
and over again in the space of a few short moments.

In addition to this,
you hear yourself giving specific instructions.

These instructions say that all directions will
not only affect you when you're in your everyday
waking state,
but will also affect you throughout your sleeping time.

You describe a picture of yourself asleep in your
bed.

You imagine there's a movie or television screen
in your mind while you are sleeping.

You now see yourself directing your mind while
you sleep.

The directions you would like your mind to
follow are playing on the screen in your mind.

You see these directions changing your life
in the way you want it changed.

As you see yourself sleeping with the screen
in your mind showing the directions you have ordered,
you are confident that,
while you sleep,
your mind is powerfully at work for you.

When you awake in the morning,
you have a tremendous sense of confidence in the
fact that you have been accomplishing something very
positive for yourself during your period of sleep.

There is yet another way in which Total Mind
Power applied to dreams can enrich your life. You
can increase your creativity by making your dreams
more beautiful, more colorful, more animated, more
wonderful and exciting even than the dreams of
your childhood.

Directing your dreams in this way gives you a
strong sense of well-being and a greater ability to cope
with the everyday world. As you realize you can
succeed in changing negative or bad dreams to happy
ones, you will become happier, more serene.

The pleasure you derive from directing your dreams
creatively and positively will cause anxieties and problems to fade away more quickly and will add a new
dimension of joy to life. This can be achieved every
night, easily, simply.

The following transcript is designed to enhance
your creativity through pleasurable dreams, thus leading
to increased pleasure and satisfaction during waking
hours:

You see yourself walking in a field of clover.

It's a warm day,
and you feel a cooling breeze on your face.

You can hear the birds singing in the nearby forest.

The sweet aroma of clover is very pleasing to you.

On your lips there's a taste of freshness from the summer day.

You feel very, very lazy, and you decide to lie down in the soft clover near a tall shade tree in the middle of the field.

After you lie down,
you start to slip into a daydreaming sleep.

It isn't an ordinary sleep,
but an extremely vivid daydream.

In this daydream you see yourself walking toward the nearby forest.

It's a deep, dark, mysterious forest,
but it does not frighten you.

You decide to enter the forest,
because it is very enchanting.

You feel compelled to follow a little path that you can see through the dense growth of trees.

As you walk through the forest,
little birds and animals scurry about you.

The forest seems friendly and protective.

There are many brightly colored,
beautiful flowers all around on the forest floor,
and lovely vines of many shades of green and brown
are entwined through the trees.

Small animals such as chipmunks and squirrels
peer at you through the undergrowth.

They're all friendly.

As you progress through the forest along the path,
you see a clearing ahead.

As you approach the clearing,
there seems to be a beautiful light filtering through
the tops of the trees.

When you arrive at the clearing,
you notice a shallow pond in front of you with
the light reflecting a spectrum of colors off the surface.

You become enchanted by the dazzling colors
that play off the surface of the pond.

The more you look at them,
the more vivid the little patterns become.

At first,
the colors are in tiny splinters of yellow,
orange and red.

As you stare at them,
the patterns of color begin to dance in your mind.

And now the colors turn a mixture of blue
and green.

The various hues seem to have a rhythm of
their own,
and,
as you contentedly watch the colors,
you begin to hear soft,
beautiful music coming through the trees.
The music seems to have a cadence in tune
with the rhythm of the dancing colors,
and you develop a feeling of exhilaration as the
patterns,
and the music,
create a wonderful,
soothing sensation in your body.

As the music continues,
you begin to feel it—as if the chords were actually
touching the skin all over your body.
You feel the music with each rhythm passing
around your body,
through your body,
and into your body.
You develop a sense of well-being that transcends
anything you have ever felt before,
and you feel as if you are part of the universe.
You feel a oneness with the world around you,
and a sense of completeness.

Now take your mind away from the colors
playing on the pond and continue through the forest.

In order to go farther,
you see that you have to take off your shoes and
wade across the shallow pond to find the path on
the other side.

You notice the graceful deer and small,
friendly animals drinking at the edges of the pond.

You feel a sense of closeness with the creatures
of the forest.

You now begin to wade across the pond,
and you can feel the soft bottom between your toes
and the cool water around your feet.

The pond seems to exert a magical effect upon you,
and you gain an overwhelming sense of well-being.

You dip your hand into the pond and take a
drink of the crystal-clear water.

It tastes so fresh and clean that you dip your
hand in repeatedly to drink from the magic pond.

You feel an added strength come over you as
you drink the water,
and you feel the magic water will benefit your health.

You develop a sense of rejuvenation and youth
that you haven't felt in a long,
long time.

You continue across the pond and find the path
that leads across the forest.

Looking down the path,
you can see that the forest soon ends and,
at the end of the trees,
there seems to be a field of beautiful flowers of
many colors.

You want to reach the field just as soon as possible.

You hurry down the path to the edge of the forest.

As you walk into the flower-covered field you
have a tremendously strong recollection of the
wonderful,
magical journey you have just been on.

You know,
however,
that the journey is not over,
because you have not returned to your field of clover.

You are really in a different field,
which gives you a sense of pleasure you haven't
experienced before.

The odors are so sweet,
so perfect,
you can taste them.

Some of the aromas seem to penetrate your body,
to give you new strength and vitality.

You walk through the field of flowers very slowly,
and pick individual flowers and deeply inhale their

wonderful fragrances.

Some flowers give you a sense of excitement,
others a sense of pleasure,
and still others a sense of floating on a cloud.

Now you continue to walk through the field
of flowers very slowly,
enjoying every moment.

At the far side of the field,
you notice another path that leads to the top of
a tall mountain.

You decide to follow the path up to the top
of the mountain,
so you can look down on all the wondrous things
you have observed during your journey.

As you go up the path you experience an
exhilaration that brings a wave of added strength.

You look forward to reaching the top of the
mountain.

The air is very fresh and clean,
and you can feel it fill your lungs with each breath
you take.

When you reach the top of the mountain
you look out over the field of flowers;
they make a beautiful,
abstract picture in your mind.

There are many,
many colors that flood your mind with lovely
sensations.

Looking back over the forest you can scarcely
see the wonderful,
enchanted pond that gave you so much pleasure
with its colors and shimmering lights.
Very,
very far away you can see the field of clover where
you started,
and it seems as if your entire spirit has been uplifted,
and that you have taken a wonderful,
enchanted journey.

You decide to leave the mountain now and
return to the field of clover where you will end your
daydreaming sleep.
There's a path that leads down the mountain
through a tangle of green and brown thicket
and brush.
The path is very clear to you,
and you seem to return to the field of clover
very quickly.
Your daydream comes to an end,
and you walk back through the field of clover
feeling totally happy and contented.

You vow that you will always be able to recall these wonderful experiences in detail whenever you wish to.

REFERENCES

Baekeland, F., Effects of Presleep Procedure and Cognitive Style on Dream Content. "Perceptual and Motor Skills," 1971, 32:63-69.

Bonime, W., "The Clinical Use of Dreams." New York: Basic Books, 1962.

Breger, L., Function of Dreams. "Journal of Abnormal Psychology," 1967, 72:1-28.

Bruce, D.J., Evans, C.R., Fenwick, P.B. and Spencer, V. Effect of Presenting Novel Verbal Material During Slow Wave Sleep. "Nature." 1970, 225:873.

Cartwright, R.D., The Influence of a Conscious Wish on Dreams: A Methodological Study of Dream Meaning and Function. "Journal of Abnormal Psychology, 1974, 83: 387-393.

Cohen, D.B., Dreaming: Experimental Investigation of Re-presentational and Adaptive Properties. In G.E. Schwartz and D. Shapiro (eds.), "Consciousness and Self-Regulation." New York: Plenum Press, 1976, 313-360.

Dallett, J., Theories of Dream Function. "Psychological Bulletin," 1973, 79:408-416.

Foulkes, D. and Rechtschaffer, A., Presleep Determinants of Dream Content: Effects of Two Films. "Perceptual and Motor Skills," 1964, 19:983-1005.

Foulkes, D. and Vogel, G., Mental Activity at Sleep Onset. "Journal of Abnormal Psychology," 1965, 70:231-243.

Hauri, P., White Noise and Dream Reporting. "Sleep Research," 1972, 1:124.

Pearlman, C.A., The Adaptive Function of Dreaming. In E. Hartman (ed.), "Sleep and Dreaming." Boston: Little, Brown, 1970.

Rechtschaffen, A., The Control of Sleep. In W.A. Hunt (ed.), "Human Behavior and Its Control." Cambridge, Mass.: Schenkman Press, 1971.

Rechtschaffen, A., The Psychophysiology of Mental Activity During Sleep. In J. McGuigan and R.A. Schoonover (eds.), "The Psychophysiology of Thinking." New York: Academic Press, 1973.

Roehrs, T., Kramer, M., Lefton, W.J., Lutz, T.E. and Roth, T., Mood Before and After Sleep. " Sleep Research," 1973, 2:95.

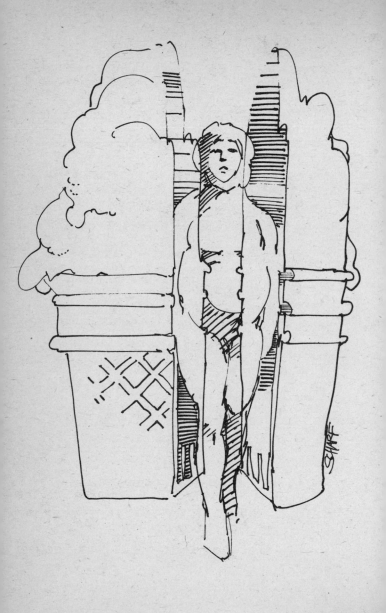

CHAPTER 10:
HOW TO CHANGE YOUR WEIGHT WITH TOTAL
MIND POWER.

Obesity has plagued humanity for thousands of years,
giving rise to an incredible number of diets and fads
reputed to be cures for the ugly problem. Drugs,
some of them dangerous, especially when used without supervision, have been developed. But the scales
continue to soar.

Some obesity may be caused by genetic problems
of metabolism or faulty glandular function and may
be tested medically, but the majority is due to over-
eating and under-exercising. Even the inherited and
glandular obesity also can be minimized by exercising
more and/or eating less.

But exerting one's often feeble will power to eat
less and to exercise more is painful, and usually a
very transient solution. Also, many overweight persons simply do not have the time to exercise properly,
so they have to eat even less to control their weight,
and the situation becomes even more painful.

However, Total Mind Power can help in a way
other methods cannot—and it doesn't require the use
of will power. Your mind, once it is directed in an

appropriate way, can decrease your desire for food, but it can also go further, and control glandular responses.

There are specific areas in your brain that control the way you metabolize food, and these you can direct. Many of them are areas being studied by medical scientists, but they are still mostly a mystery. It is also known that the glandular functions of the body are controlled from the brain. If you control your mind, you can control your glandular functions.

Total Mind Power's concepts which are not directed at determining why one overeats but rather are directed to the techniques of losing weight, are supported by the research of Dr. Albert Stunkard of the Department of Psychiatry at the University of Pennsylvania.

In a research article, "New Therapies for the Eating Disorders," Dr. Stunkard notes, "Insight therapy, with its focus on inner drives, motives, and conflicts, all too often ignores environmental factors in the control of food intake as thoroughly as does general medical treatment.

"Further, by holding out hope for an eventual solution to obesity through the resolution of conflict, it can foster magical expectations which distract the patient from more mundane concerns of greater therapeutic potential."

As you now know, Total Mind Power works to control your nervous system and thus the various parts of your body, despite the fact that you may not know what the anatomical or physiological structures look like or what their functions are. You don't have to understand them to control them, any more than we know what electricity is. You can create in your mind pictures of what you would like to have done for yourself.

You can visualize your brain as a house with little people at work, carrying out the orders you give, or whatever other concept gives you a picture of a brain at work. The important thing is for you to direct your mind along a course that will regulate the areas that control obesity.

You might picture in one area a little control switch that, when turned on, makes you hungry, and when turned off takes away your hunger. This fantasy can be as elaborate as you wish or need it to be—you can picture a pushbutton, or a toggle switch, or a huge lever or a control board. Whatever your choice, there is no need to understand the mechanics involved. You only need to know that the switch works.

The following model transcript for controlling obesity uses those visualizations as well as the other senses:

You now direct your mind to lose the weight you would like to lose.

You direct your mind to see yourself in a mirror the way you *want* to appear,
at the weight you want to be.

You see yourself removing your clothing in front of a large,
full-length mirror.

You're standing directly in front of the mirror, and there are many lights all around you,
coming from various places around the room.

As you take off articles of clothing,
you see different areas of your body that are
disgusting to you because they are fat.

One area you examine closely is your abdomen.
It seems quite large.
Even larger,
in fact,
than you imagined.

Areas such as your arms,
thighs,
neck and chin are very,
very large and protruding.

This disgusts you,
but you know you can change these things through
Total Mind Power.

Now you look into the mirror and you visualize
all of these areas of overweight melting away.

You see yourself at the wieght you would *like*
to be,
and you notice how much trimmer and better you look.

As you look at yourself in the mirror you develop
a sense of happiness and well-being that makes you
feel better than you have felt in a long,
long time.

You become very,
very proud that you have been able to lose weight.

You now have complete confidence that you
are able to do this,
and it gives you a feeling of great achievement
and satisfaction.

Now you see yourself sitting at a dining room table,
and you see various foods placed before you.
Some of these foods are quite fattening,
such as ice cream,
cakes,
bread,
cookies,
pies,
and many others you have desired in the past.
Also on the table are foods that are good for you,
such as vegetables,
meats,
cheeses,
milk,
and fruits.
You get a strong urge to eat only the foods that
are good for you,
and at the same time you want to reject the foods you
know are fattening and starchy.

Now you see yourself starting to eat some of the
foods that are good for you.
There's a piece of chicken with the fat taken off,

a raw carrot that you see yourself munching,
and other wholesome morsels.

They taste much better than the sweet and
starchy foods.

You see yourself pushing away the fattening foods.

You tell the person who put them on the table to
take them away,
because you are more interested in the foods
that are better for you.

Now you list in your mind all of the foods you
know are fattening and not good for you.

You review each and every one of them in your
mind,
in detail.

You look at them closely.

You may start out with a large chocolate ice
cream cone . . . and you see yourself losing your
taste for chocolate.

Now you see a great big whipped cream coconut
pie . . . and you see yourself losing your taste for it.

It seems too sugary and sweet,
and it tends to nauseate you a little just to think
about taking in all that sugar.

You remember hearing that many years ago
sugar was considered a powerful drug,
and only pharmacists could dispense it in small
quantities.

You decide that such a drug is not good for you in the large quantities you have been eating.

For some reason,
sugar now seems to be too much for you to tolerate, and you decide not to eat it except in very small quantities,
and only when absolutely necessary.

Now you see a huge loaf of white bread on the table.

You know it has many chemical additives in it, and all the nutrients taken out of it through processing.

You know this isn't good for you.

You see the loaf of bread,
and you think about how it would taste if you bit into it.

It appears so starchy and heavy that you just can't continue to eat such food,
so you decide you would like to give it up.

You direct your mind to tell you these things.

You visualize all of these bad foods in your mind, and you see and hear your mind telling you about each and every one of them.

You go over every item,
one by one.

Now you see some very sweet soda drinks
sitting in front of you.

They seem so sweet that if you drank them,
you would feel very,
very sick.

You see that your mind has directed you away
from all these foods you thought were tasty.

They repel you.

They are so sweet that they disgust you.

Now,
you visualize a control switch.

When turned "on," it makes you hungry;
when "off," it decreases your appetite.

You can clearly see this switch in your mind.

Whenever you want to avoid a certain food,
you see the switch turned to the "off" position.

But when the best foods are around you—in
the proper proportions—you turn the switch on,
and you eat only enough to give you adequate nutrition.

When there are sweet and starchy cakes,
pies,
candies and such foods nearby,
and you know they are not good for you,
you turn the switch off and your appetite decreases.

You direct your mind to do this each and every time food is offered to you.

You also see another switch in your mind.

This one controls the way your body metabolizes food.

This switch is turned on and left on permanently.

You see all of the little molecules and chemical particles of your body using the food you eat.

Everything you eat is metabolized and consumed in a way that does not leave you fat.

You also see a third switch that also is turned to the "on" position permanently.

This switch controls the fat cells in your body.

When the switch is on,
your mind directs the fat cells to consume all of the excess fat in your body,
and to continue consuming fat until you are the size and proportion you would like to be.

Although it is hard for an overweight person to believe, those who are underweight and unable to gain are as frustrated and exasperated as the "fatties," and often have just as hard a time.

The methods incorporated in the transcript above can be reversed for the underweight, and will work for them, whatever the cause of their thinness.

Those with illnesses such as advanced cancer may want to gain weight but find it difficult.

An athlete, or just someone anxious to build up muscles for a better physique and greater proficiency in a sport, might like to increase bulk of the nonfat variety.

The techniques of Total Mind Power may be used for these problems. The examples are merely reversed. The switches in the mind will be turned in the opposite directions. Appetite will be increased, there will be a heightened desire to eat foods known to be fattening, but of acceptable nutritional value.

It is important to remember that the mind influences the biochemical and physiological functions of your body in ways that go beyond mere suggestion— ways not yet explained by science. Therefore to gain weight you should design for yourself a transcript that directs your mind in that direction.

For example, you will picture yourself in front of a mirror, seeing yourself as you would like to be. You will describe the things you want your mind to produce, such as more muscle.

You will taste and smell the foods you direct yourself to eat, visualize your body filling out, all the muscle growing. And you will picture yourself exercising to keep your body trim and to increase your muscle strength.

According to some research studies, the act of visualizing yourself exercising may have some influence over the production or strengthening of muscle tissue. Even though this type of response is very small in measured biochemical studies, the indications are that some type of biochemical change does take place in your muscles just because you visualize them moving and being exercised.

Step Three of Total Mind Power, proper repetition, is especially valuable here. Visualizing an exercise, rather than actually doing it, takes much less time. Thus the repetition magnifies the potential for change. You can compress into a few minutes a picture, for instance, of yourself jogging around a track a hundred times, or lifting a weight a hundred times a minute, whereas the actual performance would take hours. This idea of repeating something many times over a short period may be applied to any task, such as learning to play the piano, in order to increase your proficiency.

When you make your own transcript for losing or gaining weight, be sure to bring to your aid the emotional senses as well as the five main senses and their variations. The more creative and imaginative you are, the more you impress your mind with the desired goal.

The craziest types of symbols or analogies, such as cartoon figures created by your imagination, will work. You might have little men carrying fat cells from places you don't want them and throwing them into a fire to burn up, or stringing muscles along your arms or legs where you want to increase muscle power.

Unusual and offbeat ideas are probably more effective than bland descriptions because they create more vivid pictures, and the more vivid the visualization the better your transcripts will work for you.

Since there is no practical way to prejudge the number of sessions required to accomplish your goal, a certain amount of trial and error will be necessary.

Minimum Total Mind Power sessions would be once a week at the beginning. For most people a practical and effective program is once a day for the first week, every other day during the second week, and once a week for the third week. Then, depending on the results as shown on your progress chart, you might taper off until you have accomplished your goal.

Once the goal is accomplished, you may need to return to the Total Mind Power sessions once a year, or perhaps never. The mind's potential for retaining information is tremendous, and many of your directions will be retained and acted on by the mind for years, perhaps for the rest of your life, unless you choose to change them.

REFERENCES

Abramson, E.E., A Review of Behavioral Approaches to Weight Control. "Behavior Research and Therapy," 1973, 11:547-556.

Bruch, H., "The Importance of Overweight." New York: W.W. Norton and Co., Inc., 1957.

Garb, J.R., Effectiveness of a Self-Help Group in Obesity Control. A Further Assessment. "Archives of Internal Medicine," 1974, 134:716-720.

Harris, M.B., Self-Directed Weight Control Through Eating and Exercise. "Behavior Research and Therapy," 1973, 11:523-529.

Jordan, H.A., Behavior Modification in the Treatment of Childhood Obesity. "Current Concepts in Nutrition." 1975, 3:141-150.

Mendelson, M. Psycological Aspects of Obesity. "Medical Clinics of North America," 1964, 48:1373-1385.

Musante, G.J., Obesity: A Behavioral Treatment Program. "American Family Physician," 1974, 10:95-102.

Pliner, P., Responsiveness to Affective Stimuli by Obese and Normal Individuals. "Journal of Abnormal Psychology," 1974, 83:74-80.

Schachter, S., Cognitive Effects on Bodily Functioning: Studies of Obesity and Eating. In D. Glass (ed.) "Neurophysiology and Emotion." New York: Rockefeller University Press and Russell Sage Foundation, 1967, 117-144.

Stanton, H.E., Weight Loss Through Hypnosis. "The American Journal of Clinical Hypnosis," 1975, 18:94-97.

CHAPTER 11:
INCREASING YOUR MEMORY WITH TOTAL MIND
POWER.

Memory, the ability to absorb and retain information,
is one of the necessities for survival in our society.
Our educational system requires the retention of enough
information to insure the passing of tests. The business
of making a living, in whatever field, demands some
proficiency in recalling data quickly and accurately.

Yet memory has been a problem for people for
thousands of years. The need to remember hundreds
of facts and/or figures is highly frustrating to a person
who has no trouble remembering some types of information and no talent at all for recalling others. One
person may possess an inborn ability to remember
numbers, but be totally unable to retain three items
to buy at the grocery without a list. Another may
remember names as efficiently as a computer, but
be unable to recall his own telephone number, street
address or automobile license number.

Whether you suffer from just a generally poor
memory or are deficient in isolated areas, Total Mind
Power can bring about a marked improvement for you.

I met John at a medical convention and we began
discussing new things being taught at medical school.
The young medical student told me he was very much
concerned about the enormous amount of material
covered in his classes. At the same time we discussed
studies being conducted on memory at various schools
throughout the country.

To help himself retain all the knowledge he was being taught at medical school, John said he had taken several memory courses, but found most of the codes and symbols suggested as a means of improving memory were cumbersome and almost as difficult as the subjects themselves.

Some of the techniques used, he said, such as associating a name with a dramatic story were helpful, but overall he was disappointed. I suggested some of those techniques be continued along with Total Mind Power, because they would provide him with more and better use of his mind. He agreed to try to use the methods I suggested.

Several months later, after using the techniques of Total Mind Power, John said he was able to remember details one hundred percent better than he ever had before, and with much less effort. Also, John noted that Total Mind Power had dramatically increased his confidence in his ability to handle the medical school curriculum, and as a result he was making better grades.

When you focus your awareness as in Step One, your ability to remember will increase in general. When you direct your mind to recall specific information, as you would do in Step Two, you will develop even greater ability to retain and recall facts. And this is accomplished without memory tricks, without the need for codes, symbols or other contrivances.

For instance, to increase your memory of a foreign language you are trying to learn, you would create a Step Two transcript that includes the words and phrases you want to learn. Associate these new words and phrases with as many visual and other sensory images as possible. The more unusual the associations, the more colorful they are, the more vivid will be your recollection of the words.

To illustrate, take the Spanish word "casa,"

meaning house. You might learn the word by picturing it beside the English equivalent, or by seeing it in your mind, letter by letter, with no imagery to help. But if you visualize a house with a sign on it bearing the word C-A-S-A in large letters, the association becomes more powerful.

Difficulty in remembering names is a widespread and often embarrassing problem. The Total Mind Power solution is this:

See yourself recalling the name clearly over a period of many months (compressed, of course, into a few minutes). Picture yourself meeting the person a year later and remembering the name quickly and easily. Directing your mind in this way gives you confidence in your ability to remember and a far more retentive memory as a result.

In remembering numbers, which are difficult to associate with visual or sensory imagery, direct your mind to give you a photographic memory for numbers. When you see a telephone number, direct your mind to "photograph" the whole number at a glance, rather than memorizing each digit. After a sufficient number of Step Three repetitions, you will see this remarkable new power of your mind start to work. The Total Mind Power techniques for creating a photographic memory become more and more effective with each use.

Remember, Total Mind Power techniques are to be applied according to the individual's needs. You will not remember everything that passes in front of you automatically just because you are using Total Mind Power techniques, but if there is something you want to remember, you can apply these techniques and recall it a thousand times more surely and clearly than if you were not applying Total Mind Power.

REFERENCES

Arnheim, R., "Visual Thinking." Berkeley: University of California Press, 1972.

Cohen, D.B., Toward a Theory of Dream Recall. "Psychological Bulletin," 1974c, 81:138-154.

Cohen, D.B., Dream Recall and Short Term Memory. "Perceptual and Motor Skills," 1971, 33:867-871.

Cooper, L.M., Reactivation of Memory by Hypnosis and Suggestion. "International Journal of Clinical and Experimental Hypnosis,"1973, 21:312-323.

Fowler, M.J., Sleep and Memory. "Science," 1973, 179: 302-304.

Hiscock, M. and Cohen, D.B., Visual Imagery and Dream Recall, "Journal of Research in Personality," 1973, 7:179-188.

John, E.R., Switchboard Verson Statistical Theories of Learning and Memory. "Science," 1972, 177:850-864.

John, E.R., "Mechanisms of Memory." New York: Academic Press, 1967.

Krauss, H.H., Effect of Hypnotic Time Distortion Upon Free-Recall Learning. "Journal of Abnormal Psychology, 1974, 83:140-144.

Lasaga, J. and Lasaga, A., Sleep Learning and Progressive Blurring of Perception During Sleep. "Perceptual and Motor Skills," 1973, 37:51-62.

Leiman, A.L. and Cristian, C.N., Electrophysiological Analyses of Learning and Memory. In J.A. Deutsch (ed.), "The Physiological Basis of Memory." New York: Academic Press, 1973, 160-167.

Lorayne, H. and Lucas, J., "The Memory Book." New York: Stein and Day, 1974.

Lovatt, D.J., Recall After Sleep. "American Journal of Psychology," 1968, 81:253-257.

Luria, A., "The Mind of a Mnemonist," New York: Basic Books, Inc., 1968.

Madigan, S., et. at., Picture Memory and Visual Generation Processes. "American Journal of Psychology," 87:151-158.

Marks, D.F., Visual Imagery Differences in the Recall of Pictures. "British Journal of Psychology," 1973, 64:17-24.

Roll, W.G., ESP and Memory. "International Journal of Neuropsychiatry," 1966, 2:505-521.

Samuels, S.J., Visual Recognition Memory, Paired-Associate Learning and Reading Achievement. "Journal of Educational Psychology," 1973, 65:160-167.

Seligman, M.E.P., On the Generality of the Laws of Learning. "Psychological Review," 1970, 77:406-418.

Stanford, R.G., Extrasensory Effects Upon Memory. "Journal of the American Society for Psychical Research," 1970, 64:161-186.

Stones, M.J., The Effect of Prior Sleep on Rehearsal, Recoding and Memory. "British Journal of Psychology," 1973, 64:537-543.

Straughan, J.H. and Dufort, W.H., Task Difficulty Relaxation and Anxiety Level During Verbal Learning and Recall. "Journal of Abnormal Psychology," 1969, 74:621-624.

Weiner, B., Effects of Motivation on the Availability and Retrieval of Memory Traces. "Psychology Bulletin," 1966, 65:24-37.

Wicker, F.W., Stimulus Familiarization With Pictures and Words in Paired Associate Learning. "American Journal of Psychology," 1973, 86:617-626.

Wiseman, S., Perceptual Organization as a Determinant of Visual Recognition Memory. "American Journal of Psychology," 87:675-681.

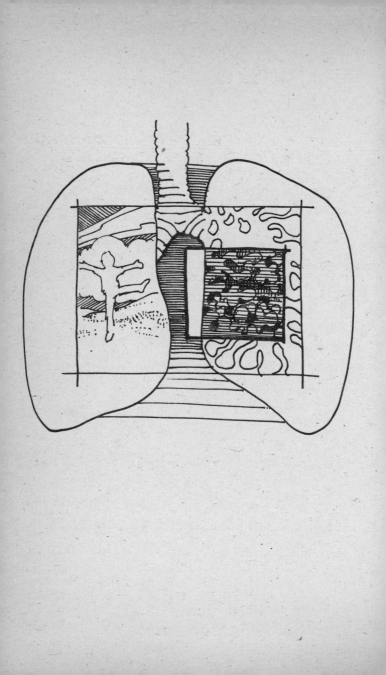

CHAPTER 12:
STOP SMOKING WITH TOTAL MIND POWER.

Smoking is one of the major health problems in the United States and throughout the world. Many have a desire to quit, but most find it nearly impossible.

Most problem smokers have tried many ways to overcome their habit—analysis, pills, group therapy. Only a handful have succeeded in ridding themselves of the habit.

A major reason for the difficulty is that smoking is more than a habit, it is a form of drug addiction, and that is very difficult to break. Will power and concentration are not effective against addiction, and self-analysis never seems to solve the problem.

Total Mind Power can be an extremely potent way to end the habit once and for all.

First, you apply Step One to focus your awareness, then you proceed to Step Two. The Step Two transcript should include such directions as these:

1. See yourself having stopped smoking and feeling very joyous that you have been able to do so.

2. Visualize situations in which you have turned down cigarettes offered to you, or avoided buying cigarettes you would ordinarily have sought.

3. Visualize yourself feeling better than you have in years as a result of having broken the smoking habit.

Build up your visualizations like a story in which you have no trouble resisting all temptation, in which you feel great satisfaction in feeling better, in no longer feeling short of breath, or having an ugly aftertaste in your mouth.

Use imagery to the maximum, in as many ways as possible. Savor your sensation of confidence that you can continue to avoid cigarette smoking as long as you like.

The success of Total Mind Power in helping you break this habit is, like its success in every area, due to it's being aimed at you, and allows for your difference from every other person.

The following transcript for breaking the smoking habit may be used as it is, or altered in any way that seems necessary to meet your specific requirements:

You picture,

on an imaginary screen in your mind,

an image of your lungs when they were pink and healthy,

as they were when you were a child.

You can see the air sacs in your lungs completely free of carbon deposits,

and you want to bring your lungs back to this
healthful state from the way they are now.

You can see your lungs expanding and contracting,
and you see that they are very efficient in their ability
to bring vital oxygen into your system.

You see yourself as a child running in a field,
and you can hear that your breathing is very natural,
very easy.

You are intrigued with the condition of your lungs,
and the perfect shape they are in.

You develop an overwhelming desire to bring
yourself back to that condition,
so you will feel healthier and able to breathe more
easily.

You now visualize your lungs the way they are
at the present time.

You see that they are very black,
and you can see carbon particles and stains covering
your lung tissues.

Many of the breathing passages are plugged off
by these deposits of black material,
and the elasticity and ability of your lungs to move
freely has been impaired.

You see yourself running in a field,
and you are very short of breath.

You have to lie down to regain your strength,
even after running just a short distance.

While you are resting in the field,
you decide that you would like to change the
condition of your lungs.

You know that smoking is one of the major
causes of the condition you are experiencing.

You also know that smoke,
when it passes through your nose,
mouth and throat,
may cause serious health problems such as cancer.

You reflect upon these thoughts and develop a
sense of urgency about stopping the use of cigarettes.

You decide to apply Total Mind Power techniques
as often as necessary to control your smoking habit.

You think about how smoking gives you a bad
taste in your mouth,
a loss of your sense of smell,
and a decreased ability to appreciate the flavor of food.

You again remember your childhood,
when foods tasted so delicious,
and you have a desire to bring these pleasures back
into your life.

You now see someone offering you a cigarette, and you see yourself refusing it.

This gives you a feeling of self-confidence about your life, so you decide to continue to refuse cigarettes that are offered to you.

Whenever you crave a cigarette, you can replace that desire by chewing a piece of sugarless gum.

You decide that you would rather keep your mouth fresh and clean than to pollute it with harmful tobacco smoke.

You now picture special blood cells circulating in all the vessels of your lung tissues, and you see these special cells attacking and dissolving the black deposits in your lungs.

You see special chemicals traveling through your blood vessels.

They dissolve in the lung tissue in order to increase the tissue's capacity and elasticity.

This makes the lungs function more completely.

You also direct your mind to send out other special chemicals that are like rejuvenating hormones.

These special chemicals help you produce new lung cells that are pink and healthy.

All of these thoughts come to you as you see
yourself lying in the field,
short of breath because of your smoking habit.

You definitely decide to produce these changes
in your life through the use of Total Mind Power.

Now you see yourself at a time when you have
completely given up your smoking habit.

You feel how much easier your breathing has
become.

You appreciate foods because of an improved
sense of taste.

You can smell beautiful aromas that you couldn't
appreciate when you were smoking.

You see yourself smelling some lovely roses,
and you see a smile coming across your face as you
fully appreciate the fragrance of the roses.

A sense of elation comes over you when you
realize that these tastes and smells are more important
to you than smoking ever was.

You visualize yourself walking along a path
that leads up a hill,
and you are amazed that you are not experiencing
shortness of breath as you always did when you
were smoking.

As you hurry up the path you come to a small mountain cafe.

You enter the cafe and talk with some of your friends who are having lunch.

One of your good friends praises you for stopping the use of cigarettes.

You feel great satisfaction.

Your friends comment that you are much less nervous than you were before,
and that you seem more relaxed.

Your friends seem genuinely excited about the big change in your life.

You're touched by the interest your friends express,
and their concern about you.

You decide to stop smoking for the rest of your life.

Specific directions to return the condition of your lungs to normal should definitely be used, especially in the light of serious problems arising from damaged lungs such as emphysema and lung cancer.

Let me emphasize again that will power, concentration, strain or effort are not necessary. Total Mind Power techniques are easy, pleasant, and they will work.

REFERENCES

Arons, H., "You Can Stop Smoking." A monograph. South Orange, N.J.: Power Publishers, Inc., 1964.

Athanasou, J., Smoking Behavior and Its Modification: A Review and Evaluation. "Terpnos Logos: The Australian Journal of Medical Sophrology and Hypnotherapy," 1974, 2:4-15.

Bernstein, D.A., Modification of Smoking Behavior: An Evaluative Review. "Psychological Bulletin," 1968, 70: 418-440.

Best, J.A., Tailoring Smoking Withdrawal Procedures to Personality and Motivational Differences. "Journal of Consulting and Clinical Psychology," 1975, 43:1-8.

Brown, B.B., Additional Characteristic EEG Differences Between Smokers and Non-Smokers. "Smoking Behavior: Motives and Incentives." Washington, D.C.: Winston & Sons, 1973.

Dengrove, E., A Single Treatment Method To Stop Smoking Using Ancillary Self-Hypnosis: Discussion. "Journal of Clinical and Experimental Hypnosis," 1970, 28:251-256.

Ferinden, W.E. and Tugender, H.S., "A Handbook of Hypno-Operant Therapy and Other Behavior Therapy Techniques, Manual No. 4 The Management of Smoking." South Orange, N.J.: Power Publishers, Inc., 1972.

Goldiamond, I., Self-Control Procedures in Personal Behavior Problems. "Psychological Reports," 1965, 17:851-868.

Guilford, J.S., "Final Report: Factors Related to Successful Abstinence from Smoking." Los Angeles: American Institutes for Research, 1966.

Greene, R.J., The Modification of Smoking Behavior by Free Operant Conditioning Methods. "Psychological Record," 1964, 14:171-178.

Heiss, J.G., "The Painless Way to Stop Smoking." Manhasset, N.Y.: Channel Press, 1962.

Hjelle, L.A. and Clouser, R., Internal-External Control of Reinforcement in Smoking Behavior. "Psychological Reports," 1970, 26:562.

Hunt, W.A., An Evaluation of Current Methods of Modifying Smoking Behavior. "Journal of Clinical Psychology," 1974, 30:431-438.

Janis, I.L. and Mann, L., Effectiveness of Emotional Role-Playing in Modifying Smoking Habits and Attitudes. "Journal of Experimental Research in Personality, 1965, 1:84-90.

Karoly, P., Effects of Outcome Expectancy and Timing of Self-Monitoring on Cigarette Smoking. "Journal of Clinical Psychology," 1975, 31:351-355.

McGall, R.M., Effect of Self-Monitoring on a Normal Smoking Behavior, "Journal of the Counseling and Clinical Psychologists," 1970, 35:135-142.

Morganstein, K.P. and Ratliff, R.G., Desensitization in Modifying Smoking Behavior. "Behaviour Research and Therapy," 1969, 7:397-398.

Pierre, R.S., Reducing Smoking Using Positive Self-Management. "Journal of School Health," 1975, 45:7-9.

Premack, D., Mechanisms of Self-Control. W. Hunt (ed.) "Learning Mechanisms of Control in Smoking." Chicago: Aldine Publishing Co., 1970.

Resnick, J.H., The Control of Smoking Behavior by Stimulus Satiation. "Behaviour Research and Therapy," 1968, 6:113-114.

Russell, M.A., Realistic Goals for Smoking and Health. A case for Safer Smoking. "Lancet," 1974, 1:254-258.

Spiegel, H.A., Single Treatment Method to Stop Smoking Using Ancillary Self-Hypnosis. "Journal of Clinical and Experimental Hypnosis," 1970, 28:235-250.

Suedfeld, P., Use of Sensory Deprivation in Facilitating the Reduction of Cigarette Smoking. "Journal of Consulting and Clinical Psychology," 1974, 42:888-895.

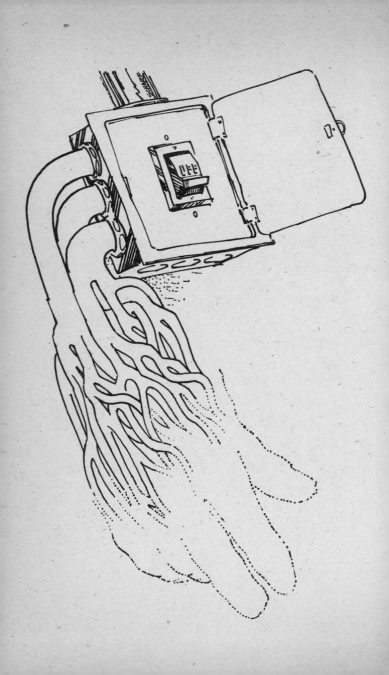

CHAPTER 13:
STOP PAIN WITH TOTAL MIND POWER.

There are hundreds of creditable theories about what causes pain, and easily thousands of techniques for alleviating it. But most of these require prescriptions and medical supervision. Many require hospitalization. Thus the individual who is away from a physician or hospital has few options beyond suffering and making the best of it.

The contemporary belief is that, in very complex ways, pain sensations travel a path of nerves from the brain to other parts of the body. Some theories hold that pain is a learned response.

Certainly the mind has considerable influence over pain responses, even in those who do not consciously try to control it. The witch doctors of certain cultures use trance states, and even physicians of ancient times used trance-like states or other methods of distraction to help control pain. History shows that the ability of the mind to control pain was accepted thousands of years ago. You yourself have probably had the experience of being unaware of pain

119

while concentrating deeply—perhaps you were trying to rescue someone from a fire, and only became aware of the pain of your own burns after the rescue was over—because your mind had been so completely centered on the task at hand.

Total Mind Power is highly effective in controlling pain, and requires no medication, no prescriptions, not even the presence of another person. Wherever you are, under whatever circumstances, you can apply Total Mind Power.

A young woman came into my office with a large skin tumor on her back. It had a malignant appearance which tests later substantiated, and definitely had to be removed. When I explained the situation to her, she became hysterical and refused treatment because of her fear of pain. She had experienced several painful dental sessions and had become extremely sensitive to such procedures.

Because the problem was serious and surgery seemed imperative, I gave the young woman instructions for using Total Mind Power techniques, to be used daily for five minutes before bedtime for one week, to prepare her for painless surgery at the end of the week.

She didn't believe at all that the techniques would help her, but because of the nature of the problem she agreed to do as I had asked. A week later she came into my office for the surgery, calm and ready to accept the fact that the operation would have to be performed. In fact, she was so confident she did not believe she needed even a local anesthetic.

The skin tumor was removed very easily, with about one-fourth the quantity of local anesthetic usually required, and she recovered rapidly and completely.

Most persons visiting a doctor's office are totally

unaware that their minds can change their pain responses and in many cases block all pain from whatever procedure needs to be performed.

The Step Two transcripts you create for stopping pain will almost certainly be incorrect in a medical or anatomical sense, but that is unimportant as long as they make sense to you, making it possible to provide for your mind graphic directions it can understand and use to cut off pain from any part of your body.

If you were scheduled to have a skin tumor removed surgically from your right hand, you might visualize wire-like nerves leading from that hand, the wires resembling electrical or telephone wires.

You see the wires winding up along the length of your arm and through your shoulder and neck. As they approach the brain the wires become noticeably thicker, enabling them to carry more information. These, of course, represent the nerves you are concerned with. At their thickest part, just before they enter the brain, they go through a switch box equipped with a lever for turning "current" on or off. The off position stops any signal from traveling through the wire as surely as if you turned off an electric light switch. This is the basis for the Step Two transcript you will prepare for easing the pain of the operation.

The transcript would describe in detail all the nerve-like wires, their color, size, the exact path they follow. You would describe the intricate details of the switch box. Every rivet and terminal would be clearly visible in your mind's eye, as would the working of the switch that, in the off position, blanks out the transmission of impulses along the wires. Even the temperature around the wires would be pictured—use all your senses to reinforce the impressions.

Several days before the removal of the tumor is

scheduled, practice turning the switch on and off at will. As you continue repetitions (Step Three) you will begin to notice increasing numbness in your hand each time you turn the switch off. Just before the surgery, turn the switch off and leave it in that position.

This same nerve and switch concept can be used for controlling pain in conjunction with transcripts designed to deal with particular illnesses causing pain, so that actually two or three Step Two transcripts are woven together.

You might, for example, incorporate into a transcript dealing with arthritis the technique of closing the switch to shut off the pain impulse from the affected joint, plus directions for your mind to send out special antibody fighters from the brain, through the affected areas, to fight the inflammation.

Whether or not the concepts are medically correct is not relevant. The important thing is that your mind is directed toward accomplishing the end result you want. If you are under medical treatment for the condition, get as much information about your condition as possible from your doctor and add it to the transcript, so your mind and his treatment can work together.

As you can see, the applications of Total Mind Power are limitless. Everyone needs, at some time in life, to find a technique for fighting pain, disease, fear or other difficulty. Whatever your problem is, Total Mind Power can be applied and will help. Anyone can use Total Mind Power, whether the problem is simple or complex.

REFERENCES

Barber, T.X., Implications for Capabilities and Potentialities: Control of Pain. "Biofeedback and Self Control 1974," 1975, 5:53-54.

Benson, H., Klemchuk, M.P. and Graham, J.R., The Use-fulness of the Relaxation Response in the Therapy of Head-ache. "Headache," 1974, 14:49-52.

Blitz, B. and Dinnerstein, A.J., Role of Attentional Foucs in Pain Perception: Manipulation of Response to Noxious Sti-mulation by Instruction. "Journal of Abnormal Psychology," 1971, 77:42-45.

Bobey, M.J. and Davidson, P.O., Psychological Factors Af-fecting Pain Tolerance. "Journal of Psychosomatic Research," 1970, 14:370-376.

Budzinski, T., Stoyva, J. and Adler, C., Feedback-Induced Muscle Relaxation: Application to Tension Headache. "Journal of Behavior Therapy and Experimental Psychiatry," 1970, 1:205-211.

Evans, F.J., The Placebo Response in Pain Reduction. "Biofeedback and Self-Control." 1975. 5:72-79.

Gannon, L. and Sternbach, R.A., Alpha Enhancement as a Treatment for Pain: A Case Study. "Journal of Behavior Therapy and Experimental Psychiatry," 1971, 2:209-213.

Green, R.J. and Reyher, J., Pain Tolerance in Hypnotic Analgesic and Imgaination States. "Journal of Abnormal Psychology," 1972, 79:29-38.

Hay, K.M., Migraine Treated by Relaxation Therapy. "Journal of the Royal College of General Practioners," 1971, 21:664-669.

Haynes, S.N., Griffin, P., Mooney, D. and Parise, M., Electromyographic Biofeedback and Relaxation Instructions in the Treatment of Muscle Contraction Headaches. "Behavior Therapy," 1975, 6:672-678.

Mitchell, K.R., A Psychological Approach to the Treatment of Migraine. "British Journal of Psychiatry," 1971, 119: 533-534.

Mitchell, K.R. and Mitchell, D.M.., Migraine: An Exploratory Treatment Application of Programmed Behavior Therapy Techniques. "Journal of Psychosomatic Reserach," 1971, 15:137-157.

Nisbett, R.E. and Schachter, S., Cognitive Manipulation of Pain. "Journal of Experimental Social Psychology," 1966, 2:227-236.

Sargent, J.D., Green, E.E. and Walters, E.D., The Use of Auto-genic Feedback Training in a Pilot Study of Migraine and Tension Headaches. "Headache," 1972, 12:120-124.

Sargent, J., Walters, D. and Green, E., Psychosomatic Self-Regulation of Migraine and Tension Headaches. "Seminars in Psychiatry," 1973, 5:415-428.

Spanos, N.P., Barber, T.X. and Lang, G., Cognition and Self-Control: Cognitive Control of Painful Sensory Input. In H. London and R.E. Nisbett (eds.), "Thought and Feeling: Cognitive Alteration of Feeling States." Chicago: Aldine, 1974, 141-158.

Tasto, D.L., Muscle Relaxation Treatment for Tension Headaches. "Behavior Research and Therapy," 1973, 11:347-349.

CHAPTER 14:
HOW TO IMPROVE SPORTS PERFORMANCE WITH
TOTAL MIND POWER.

The phenomenon of "choking under pressure" is well
known to amateur and professional athletes alike. A
service return or a two-foot put, whether it's for a
$50,000 purse or a beer, can be vital, and the know-
ledge that it is can tense the player so he flubs the
shot.

The psychological factor can play as important
a part in sports performance as skill; it can be the
final determinant of victory or defeat.

Total Mind Power, applied to sports performance,
helps in both areas, improving your ability to overcome psychological problems and enabling you to increase your skill. A major sports magazine reported
recently that a professional golfer, one of the con-
sistent top-money winners on tour, uses visualization
to insure perfect shots. In his mind he pictures the
trajectory of the ball; he also picutres the colors of
the flag and pin, and uses every other sensory system
to get the winning result.

Your individual performance can be improved in
the same way, perhaps at tennis, rapidly becoming the
most popular sport for singles and families. Increasing

your skill at the game through Total Mind Power is dependent upon directing your mind to perform the particular tennis strokes that need improvement in exactly the correct way. You visualize yourself performing precisely as you should.

If you are having trouble with a particular stroke, develop a transcript incorporating every detail of that stroke as it is correctly executed. You may get your information through lessons from a professional teacher, or from one of the many books on how to play tennis. If practical, incorporate the step-by-step directions into your Step Two recording. The mechanics of the stroke can be repeated several times, with emphasis on a different facet of the stroke each time.

Include as many sensory experiences as possible. In addition to the description of the perfect stroke, include a visualization of yourself hitting the ball properly, the ball traveling across the net and landing in the proper spot on the court. Hear the sound of the ball striking your racquet; describe your feeling of pride of accomplishment in the performance. You might even picture yourself playing in a tournament, making the perfect shot, and earning the applause of the watching crowd. Think of the smell of the sun-warmed court, and any other sensory details that will strengthen the impact.

Most persons have more trouble with the backhand stroke than the forehand, although this is anatomically illogical, because the backhand is actually an easier stroke than the forehand. The following transcript should help you develop a more powerful backhand. Use the transcript after you have used your Step One transcript for focusing awareness.

This transcript is for a right-handed person. If you are left-handed, the words left and right may be reversed:

You see yourself watching the tennis ball approach
your backhand side.

As it crosses the net,
you see yourself bring your racquet back with its
head dropping below your waist.

You now see your right foot step over and
point to the left side of the court.

You feel the weight of your body shift to your
right foot as you make contact with the outside
undersurface of the ball.

Your stroke moves smoothly forward.

You see your racquet meeting the ball out in
front of you,
just before it reaches your right hip.

You see yourself watching the ball intently.

You can even see it sink into the taut racquet
strings,
compress,
then travel back toward the top of the net as you
complete the stroke.

You feel the head of the racquet move around
your body and stop at your right side.

When the racquet contacts the ball,
you visualize the muscles in your forearm.

The muscles of your wrist and fingers hold the
racquet very firmly,
and perpendicular to the court surface.

Now you see the ball traveling to a precise spot
you have chosen on your opponent's side.

You feel a tremendous wave of excitement and
joy at this uncanny accuracy.

The ball is returned repeatedly by your opponent
to your backhand side,
and you see yourself returning the ball perfectly each
time.

It travels to the exact spot you select,
without exception.

Each time you hit the ball you see in detail each
and every move you make,
and the moves flow together to create a vivid
picture of your perfect backhand stroke.

You now visualize a professional tennis player
you have seen play.

You see this player hitting a perfect backhand
stroke,
and you imagine that *you* are that player,
competing in a major tournament.

You picture the last crucial point of the match
as a backhand shot you hit perfectly.

You hear the crowd applaud and cheer wildly,
and you enjoy the praise and admiration given to you.

You now see yourself hitting that same perfect

shot one thousand times in the next few minutes.

You observe and sense every fine detail of the shot.

You hear the gratifying sound of the tennis ball
meeting the head of the racquet in its exact center.

You feel your feet move on the court with
absolute precision,
enabling you to meet the ball at the precise moment
it should be hit.

You hear the whiz of the ball,
and you feel the motion of the air around you
as you complete your perfect swing.

You feel yourself becoming exhilarated as you
hit shot after shot with your flawless backhand stroke.

Now you see yourself in a hard-fought tennis
match,
and your opponent keeps hitting hard shots to your
backhand side.

Each time the ball comes at you across the net,
you tell yourself that you'll hit a perfect backhand
return.

You feel and hear yourself saying this hundreds
of times in just a few short moments as the match
progresses.

Finally,
you hit the last stroke of the match with a perfect
backhand drive,

and you gain a confidence and power in your tennis
game that gives you tremendous satisfaction and
pleasure.

You see yourself being rewarded for your tennis
performance as people come up to congratulate you.

You develop a pride and confidence in your
game,

and you are elated to know that you can apply
Total Mind Power techniques to improve your other
strokes as well.

REFERENCES

Bankov, M., Autogenic Training, Hypnosis, Revelation and
Psychotherapy Modeling as Psychoprophylactic and Psycho-
therapueutic Methods for Athletes. "Psychotherapy and
Psychosomatics," 1972-73, 21:62-66.

Basmajian, J.V., Electromyography Comes of Age. The Conscious Control of Individual Motor Units in Man May be Used
to Improve His Physical Performance. "Science," 1972, 176:
603-609.

Bilodeau, E.A. (ed.), "Principles of Skill Acquisition."
New York: Academic Press, 1969.

Blum, G.S., Effects of the Restriction of Conscious Awareness in a Reaction Time Tast. "International Journal of
Clinical and Experimental Hypnosis," 1974, 22:335-345.

Butler, K.N., The Effect of Physical Conditioning and Exertion on the Performance of a Simple Mental Task. "Journal
of Sports Medicine," 1969, 9:236-240.

Chaney, D.S., Relaxation and Neuromuscular Tension Control and Change in Motor Performance Under Induced
Tension. "Perceptual and Motor Skills," 1973, 36:185-186.

Erickson, M.H. and Erickson, E.M., Further Considerations
of Time Distortion-Time Condensation and Expansion.
"American Journal of Clinical Hypnosis, 1958, 1:83-88.

Fetz, E. and Finocchio, D.V., Operant Conditioning of
Specific Patterns of Neural and Muscular Activity.
"Science," 1971, 174:431-435.

Gallway, W.T., "The Inner Game of Tennis." New York: Random House, 1974.

Genova, E., Changes in Certain Physical Functions Affected by Autogenous Relaxation. "Journal of Sports Medicine and Physical Fitness," 1973, 13:125-130.

Kahneman, D., "Attention and Effort." Englewood Cliffs, N.J.: Prentice-Hall, 1973.

McKenzie, T.L., Effects of Self-Recording on Attendance and Performance in a Competitive Swimming Training Environment. "Journal of Applied Behavior Analysis," 1974, 7:199-206.

Morgan, W.P., Psychological Factors Influencing Perceived Exertion. "Medicine and Science in Sports," 1973, 5:97-103.

Nideffer, R.M. and Deckner, C.W., A Case Study of Improved Athletic Performance Following Use of Relaxation Procedures. "Perceptual and Motor Skills," 1970, 30:821-822.

O'Brien, M., The Effects of Positive and Negative Reinforcement in Manual Dexterity Testing. "Journal of Clinical Psychology," 1975, 31:74-77.

Paben, M. and Rosentswieg, J., Control of Muscular Tension in Learning a Novel Gross Motor Skill. "Perceptual and Motor Skills," 1971, 32:556-558.

Parker, P.D. and Barber, T.X., Hypnosis, Tast Motivating Instructions, and Learning Performance. "Journal of Abnormal and Social Psychology," 1964, 69:499-504.

Rushall, B.S., The Status of Personality Research and Application in Sports and Physical Education. "Journal of Sports Medicine and Physical Fitness," 1973, 13:281-290.

Scully, H.E. and Basmajian, J.V., Motor-Unit Training and Influence of Manual Skill. "Psychophysiology," 1969, 5:625-632.

Simard, T.G. and Basmajian, J.V., Methods in Training the Conscious Control of Motor Units. "Archives of Physical Medicine," 1967, 48:12-19.

CHAPTER 15:
HOW TO USE TOTAL MIND POWER TO BRING YOU BETTER HEALTH.

When Total Mind Power is applied to a specific problem, it tends not only to solve that problem, but also to bring the bonus of an overall feeling of improved health and well-being. This feeling can be enhanced by directing your mind to improvement in these areas even when you have no particular health or other problems needing attention.

A recent research paper by Dr. Gary E. Schwartz, Harvard University assistant professor of Personality Psychology, states, "By training subjects to control voluntarily combinations of visceral, neural and motor responses, it is possible to assess linkages between physiological responses and their relationship to human consciousness."

Similar positions on the ability of the human mind to influence bodily functions are being published in scientific literature around the world. Total Mind Power's essence is derived from such research allowing individuals to benefit from published scientific studies.

132

The following model transcript is designed to serve this purpose, thus adding to the pleasure of your everyday life. Its use also may slow down the aging process as well as ward off some diseases:

You visualize yourself youthful and vigorous,
the way you want to be.

You continue to focus this picture in your mind as you turn your awareness to your health.

You will feel a new energy and vitality in your life through the use of Total Mind Power.

Your nervous system will become more stable, and you will feel much less anxiety than before.

All the systems of your body will begin to function at higher levels as you direct your mind to improve your life.

Your entire metabolism will become more attuned to your needs.

Your digestive system will use the food you eat more completely.

You will limit your consumption of food to just the quantities you need to give you proper nutrition.

You will desire only the foods you know are good for you.

Because you are developing a more relaxed and

less anxious outlook toward life and your surroundings,
you will find that you have more time to eat and
digest your food properly.

Your metabolism during rest will be more natural,
and will be adjusted for your relaxed state.

Because of the improvement in your metabolism,
you will develop a more natural heart rate,
and your breathing rate will become more natural
by virtue of increased oxygen intake due to better
performance of your lungs.

Your entire nervous system will function more
efficiently.

Your automatic nervous system (technically
known as the autonomic nervous system),
which controls your heart rate and many other vital
functions without your conscious awareness,
will work in a more natural and health-giving manner.

Because of this improvement in your nervous
system,
your digestion and kidney functions,
which are largely controlled by your autonomic
nervous system,
will improve tremendously.

Your blood supply to vital organs,
such as your liver,
spleen and pancreas,

will nourish those organs more effectively.

All the chemistry in your body will become more balanced.

And the physiological changes of your body will become more natural.

Your brain waves will become more and more balanced,
indicating a more peaceful and restful nature.

Because of this balancing of your brain waves, you will sleep more deeply and dream more beautiful dreams.

The improved balance of your biochemical and metabolic system will increase your general resistance to diseases and infections.

Because of the stability of your nervous system, your blood pressure will remain normal,
and you'll be able to maintain your proper weight more easily.

The tone of your muscles will improve,
and you will find that you have more energy and strength with which to carry out your everyday tasks.

Your ability to tolerate extreme heat or cold improves,

because you are able to control the blood supply to your skin more efficiently.

The texture and appearance of your skin takes on new life.

You notice an increased luster and body to your hair.

The reaction time of your reflexes improves, and you have the ability to shift the focus of your eyes more rapidly.

You direct your mind to improve all of these areas as you use Total Mind Power to change and control your life.

Your mental functions also should improve as a result of this particular application of Total Mind Power. Biochemical and metabolic functions are thought to be linked to mental performance. Therefore, when one is improved, improvement in the other should follow. Enhanced feelings of well-being also contribute to sharper mental capacity.

Through application of Total Mind Power, every facet of your life should improve immeasurably, and without effort or strain. You will find yourself experiencing better sports performance, deeper sleep, a better outlook on life, more satisfactory social relationships, and a greater joy in living.

REFERENCES

Borkovec, T.D., Kaloupek, D.E. and Slama, K., The Facilitative Effect of Muscle Tension Release in the Relaxation and Treatment of Sleep Disturbance. "Behavior Therapy," 1975, 6:301-309.

Borkovec, T.D., Physiological and Cognitive Processes in the Regulation of Anxiety. In G.E. Schwartz and D. Shapiro (eds.), "Consciousness and Self-Regulation." New York: Plenum Press, 1976, 261-312.

Bradley, R.A. (ed.), The Dimensions of Healing: A Symposium. "The Academy of Parapsychology and Medicine," 1973.

Dorsey, J.M., Etiology and Treatment of Emotional Factors in Allergic Diseases. "Annals of Allergy, 1972, 30:223.

Edelman, R.J., Effects of Progressive Relaxation on Autonomic Processes. "Journal of Clinical Psychology." 1970, 26:421-425.

Freeling, N.W., The Psychophsiological Effects of Brief Relaxation Training: A test of the Maximal Habituation Hypothesis. "Dissertation Abstracts International," 1972, 32:4856-4857.

French, A.P., Therapeutic Application of a Simple Relaxation Method. "American Journal of Psychotherapy," 1974, 28:287.

Grace, W.J. and Graham, D.T., Relationship of Specific Attitudes and Emotions to Certain Bodily Diseases. "Psychosomatic Medicine," 1952, 14:253-261.

Green, E.E., Green, A.M. and Walters, E.D., Voluntary Control of Internal States: Psychological and Physiological. "Journal of Transpersonal Psychology," 1970, 2:1-25.

Jacobson, E., Neuromuscular Controls in Man: Methods of Self-Direction in Health and Disease. "American Journal of Psychology," 1955, 68:549-561.

Mallory, M.T., Mind Over Body. "National Observer," 1973, 12:1-10.

Miller, N.E., Learning Viseral and Glandular Responses. "Science." 1969, 163:434-445.

Pines, M., Train Yourself to Stay Well. "McCall's," 1970, 48:137-138.

Schwartz, G.E., Biofeedback, Self-Regulation, and the Patterning of Physiological Processes. "American Scientist," 1975, 63:314-324.

Shaprio, D., Operant Conditioning: A New Theoretical Approach in Psychosomatic Medicine. "International Journal of Psychiatry in Medicine," 1974, 5:377-387.

Solomon, G.F. and Moos, R.H., Emotions, Immunity and Disease. "Archives of General Psychiatry," 1964, 11:657-674.

Walrath, L.C., Autonomic Correlates of Meditation and Hypnosis. "American Journal of Clinical Hypnosis," 1975, 170:190-197.

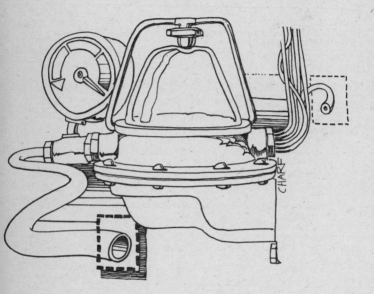

CHARF

CHAPTER 16:
LOWERING HIGH BLOOD PRESSURE WITH
TOTAL MIND POWER.

High blood pressure accounts for many deaths every
year, from related strokes and heart attacks. Many
of the drugs that control high blood pressure present
dangers in themselves, and have side effects that
patients find unpleasant, so that sustained taking of
the needed drugs is often refused.

Total Mind Power can have a major and lasting
influence on combating high blood pressure and on
the quantity and types of medication required. For
some, it may eliminate the need for the drugs.

Research, by such distinguished scientists as Dr.
Donald A. Kristt at Johns Hopkins University School
of Medicine, indicates the mind can be directed toward
the reduction of blood pressure.

In a research article Dr. Kristt states, "The results
of this study confirm and substantially extend the
findings . . . that patients with high blood pressure can
learn to lower their Systolic Blood Pressure while in
the laboratory." Also, Dr. Kristt's findings show the
effectiveness of the skills learned in the laboratory

can have influence on blood pressure for at least three months.

This chapter discusses the Total Mind Power techniques which can aid you in controlling high blood pressure.

This is not to say that an individual should not seek medical care. Total Mind Power may be used along with any treatments that are being prescribed and for those persons who have "gone off" prescribed medicines because of their side effects, Total Mind Power should be used as often as possible to reduce the blood pressure.

A situation I recall concerns Harry, a healthy-appearing, middle-aged man who came to my office for a problem that required a type of medication known to cause side affects that included raising the blood pressure for a short time.

I asked Harry if he ever had high blood pressure and he replied he had had it for several years but never seemed able to take the medications to control it. Why hadn't Harry been able to take the medicines? He said they made him feel "peculiar" and even impotent.

From a medical viewpoint I could appreciate Harry's concerns about taking the medicines, but I also realized he was taking a risk in not treating the high blood pressure which eventually could make him another fatality of this disease.

While he seemed doubtful at first, after explaining research that had been conducted in the use of the mind to control blood pressure, Harry agreed to learn the techniques of Total Mind Power and apply them to his problem. After all, if he was reluctant to use medications, which he said made him feel "peculiar," then he had nothing to lose and much to gain in his fight against high blood pressure.

After several weeks use of Total Mind Power he had lowered his blood pressure to normal and has been able to maintain a normal blood pressure with intermittent use thereafter.

The results from the use of Total Mind Power are easily measured, because a physician, or even a properly instructed individual at home can, in a few minutes, determine how blood pressure is doing. You monitor your progress and as your blood pressure responds you increase or decrease the frequency of your application of Total Mind Power. Since each person is different, it is important that you apply Total Mind Power for yourself, according to your own needs and personality.

The Step Two transcript you make for controlling blood pressure could include these points:

Visualize the blood vessels in your body leading into a pump that represents your heart.

The blood vessels you see at first are extremely narrow and very tight.

The pump is working unusually hard to get the blood through them,
and its pressure gauge is very high,
in the red danger zone.

You direct your mind to relax the tight blood vessels,
and you immediately see them relax and open up.

They increase noticeably in size,
the blood courses through them,
and the pressure gauge drops down from the danger zone into the safe green area.

Describe all of this in the most detailed and precise manner, introducing as many sensory details as possible.

If you are undergoing treatment for your condition, ask your doctor for as many details as possible about causes and mechanisms. As many descriptive details as practical should be used to speed the improvement, perhaps even eliminate the basic cause, or at least reinforce his treatment.

However, even if very little is known about the causes or mechanisms of your condition, and if you do not at a given moment have access to a doctor, Total Mind Power can help you. Make your transcript in any way you believe will be most helpful, creating cartoon-like pictures if that is what will impress your mind the most at the moment.

Wherever you are, you can use Total Mind Power. If you do not have a recorder, read your transcript to yourself. And remember that doing so just before going to sleep brings an added bonus of reinforcement to your technique.

REFERENCES

Benson, H., Marzetta, B.R. and Rosner, B.A., Decreased Blood Pressure Associated With the Regular Elicitation of the Relaxation Response: A Study of Hypertensive Subjects. "Stress and the Heart," 1974, 1:293-302.

Benson, H., Shapiro, D., Tursky, B. and Schwartz, G.E., Decreased Systolic Blood Pressure Through Operant Conditioning Techniques in Patients With Essential Hypertension. "Science," 1971, 173:740-741.

Deabler, H.L., The Use of Relaxation and Hypnosis in Lowering High Blood Pressure. "American Journal of Clinical Hypnosis," 1973, 16:75-83.

Frederick, A.N. and Barber, T.X., Yoga, Hypnosis and Self-Control of Cardiovascular Functions. "Proceedings of the Annual Covention of the Psychological Association," 1971, 7:859-860.

Gutmann, M.C. and Benson, H., Interaction of Environmental Factors and Systematic Arterial Blood Pressure: A Review. "Medicine," 1971, 50:543-553.

Harris, R.E. and Singer, M.T., Interaction of Personality and Stress in the Pathogenesis of Essential Hypertension. "Hypertension, Proceedings of the Council of High Blood Pressure Research," 1967, 16:104-115.

Keegan, D.L. Psychosomatics: Toward an Understanding of Cardiovascular Disorders. "Psychosomatics," 1973, 14: 321-325.

Kezdi, P., Neurogenic Control of the Blood Pressure in Hypertension. "Cardiologia," 1967, 51:193-203.

Korner, P.I., Central Nervous Control of Autonomic Function: Possible Implications in the Pathogenesis of Hypertension. "Circulation Research," 1970, 27:159-168.

Kristt, D.A., Learned Control of Blood Pressure in Patients with High Blood Pressure. "Circulation," 1975, 51:370-378.

Miller, N.E., DiCara, L.V., Solomon, H., Weiss, J.M. and Dworkin, B., Psychological Aspects of Hypertension. Learned Modifications of Autonomic Functions: A Review and Some New Data. "Circulation Research, Supplement No. 1, July 1970.

Patel, C., Twelve-Month Follow Up of Yoga and Biofeedback in the Management of Hypertension. "Lancet," 1975, Vol. 62.

Patel, C.H., Yoga and Biofeedback in the Management of Hypertension. "Lancet," November 1973, 1053-1055.

Redmon, D.P., Blood Pressure and Heart-Rate Response to Verbal Instruction and Relaxation in Hypertension. "Psychosomatic Medicine," 1974, 36:285-297.

Shapiro, D., Tursky, B., Gershon, E. and Stern, M., Effects of Feedback and Reinforcement on the Control of Human Systolic Blood Pressure. "Science," 1969, 163:588-590.

Shapiro, D., Schwartz, G.E. and Tursky, B., Control of Diastolic Blood Pressure in Man by Feedback and Reinforcement. "Psychophysiology," 1972, 296-304.

Shoemaker, J.E., The Effects of Muscle Relaxation on Blood Pressure of Essential Hypertensives. "Behaviour Research and Therapy," 1975, 13:29-43.

Thomas, C.B., The Psychological Dimensions of Hypertension. "The Epidemiology of Hypertension," 1967, 332-339.

The Human Eye

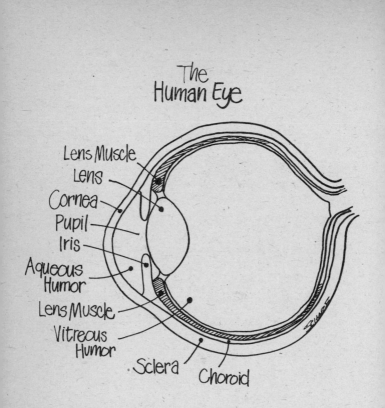

Lens Muscle
Lens
Cornea
Pupil
Iris
Aqueous Humor
Lens Muscle
Vitreous Humor
Sclera
Choroid

CHAPTER 17:
HOW TO IMPROVE YOUR EYESIGHT WITH TOTAL MIND POWER.

Although man has been suffering from eye problems since the beginning of history, many of the mechanisms causing poor vision still are not understood, and the cause of some problems is still unidentified.

It is known that some visual difficulties are caused by distortion of the eyeball and lens, and that muscles surrounding the eyeball have an influence on the contour. In some cases exercises to strengthen and control eye muscles have improved the vision of nearsighted or farsighted persons.

Internal eyeball pressure affects vision; natural aging alters it; astigmatism, an unusual shape of the eyeball, causes distortion; high blood pressure and other illnesses affect the way you see.

However, application of Total Mind Power to improvement of your vision does not require understanding of the causes of the problem or of how the eye works. As long as you can visualize something understandable to you, you will be able to direct your mind to improve the situation.

You might imagine, for example, that your eye lenses are controlled by an ordinary workshop vise. When you tighten or loosen the vise, the lens becomes thicker or thinner. Your mind will know what this symbolizes and will go to work on the problem; no technical knowledge is necessary.

It will be helpful, though, especially if you are being treated for your eye difficulty, to get as much information as possible from your doctor. This will make it easier to create a transcript that will help you take part in the doctor's therapy.

Scientific knowledge of the mind's ability to control near or farsightedness, or any other health problem, is incomplete, but indications are that the mind has tremendous influence over bodily functions. This chapter, like all the chapters in this book, seeks to supply you with a framework to guide you in using your mind more completely than ever before to improve your health and your life.

The following Step Two transcript may be used as it is, or as a model on which to create one that applies more specifically to your individual difficulty:

You picture in your mind a diagram of your eyes.

You see the lenses that do the job of focusing on the objects you look at.

These lenses can be adjusted automatically by your mind.

They focus images onto the back part of your eye,
similar to the way a magnifying glass focuses an image.

You know that if the lenses are distorted in any manner,

the images will be out of focus.

You picture special muscles around the lenses
which,
when contracted or relaxed,
change the thickness of the lenses,
thus changing the focus of objects at which you look.

If you are nearsighted,
you direct your mind to tighten the muscles around
the lenses of your eyes in order to thin out the lenses.

You would then see distant objects more clearly.

If you are farsighted,
you see the muscles around the lenses relaxing to
make the lenses thicker.

This brings nearby objects into more perfect focus.

If your eyes are shaped incorrectly,
the images your lenses focus will be indistinct.

You direct your mind to contract or relax the
muscles that are attached to your eyes in order to
give the correct shape to your eyes.

If you have cataracts (cloudiness of the eye lenses),
direct your mind to send special chemicals through
your blood stream into your eyes.

These chemicals dissolve into the lenses of your

eyes and eliminate the particles in your lenses.

As your vision improves,
you develop a sense of relief in knowing that you are
able to see better than ever before.

You decide that you will use these Total Mind
Power techniques as often as necessary to maintain
your improved vision.

You picture the nerves that go into the back of
your eyes and connect with your brain.

These nerves pick up signals from the objects
you look at.

You direct your mind to have these nerves
pick up the focused images from your lenses in a
more precise fashion.

If you have other diseases affecting your eyes,
you direct your mind to send chemicals through your
blood stream to your eyes to clear up these diseases.

You now see yourself having your eyes tested,
and you hear your doctor commenting on the improvement in your eyesight.

You are elated to know that your mind can control and change your visual problems.

Now you visualize a stage on which a play
is taking place.

You see yourself sitting in the audience watching
the play.

Between acts,
a performer holds up a sign that shows the title
of the next act.

At first,
the printing on the sign seems to be out of focus,
but you direct your mind to control the muscles
of your eyes to bring the printing into sharper focus.

During the play you begin to see the performers
much more clearly than before,
and you can visualize every detail of what is occurring
on the stage.

You adjust your eyesight to pick up all the
details of the play,
and you become more adept at rapidly focusing
your eyes.

You enjoy the performance,
and you develop total confidence in your ability
to adjust your vision for whatever situation occurs.

You again see yourself in your doctor's office,
and you are taking an eye test.

There is a large eye chart at the far end of the
room,

and you imagine yourself reading the letters.

You find that when you come to a letter you cannot see clearly,
you adjust the focus of your eyes to bring the letter in more clearly.

You do this by simply thinking about the muscles that control your eyes.

You are quite pleased with yourself,
because you are able to see easily letters that were previously blurred.

Now you see yourself in a library that displays hundreds of posters about current books.

When you look at the posters you find you are able to focus your eyes precisely on the lettering.

Even small letters that you ordinarily have difficulty seeing are in sharp focus.

Some of the posters have pictures of people and animals on them,
and you can also focus these images more clearly than before.

You can feel and sense the muscles of your eyes controlling the shape of your eyeballs and the contours of your lenses.

You hear your own voice complimenting you on your ability to control your vision so effectively.

You now see a cartoon-like picture of your eyes.

You may see them as movie cameras with gears, lenses and wheels,

or in any other way comfortable to you.

Whatever your eye condition may be,

you direct your mind to send out animated cartoon characters who are miniature eye doctors.

These little doctors work on the areas of your eyes that are problems to you.

If you have cloudiness of the inner fluid of your eyes,

you see these doctors bring in special containers

to collect the cloudy material suspended in the fluid.

If you have a problem with the shape of your eyes or your lenses,

you see the doctors using special instruments to shape and correct these irregularities.

After they have removed the problems,

they add fresh eye fluid,

and your vision improves dramatically.

You may also picture the doctors repairing

the nerves and blood vessels of your eyes if you have a problem in those areas.

You hear the doctors talking about what they are doing to repair your eyes.

Now you see yourself with phenomenal eyesight.

You see yourself reading books,

looking at distant objects,

and reading far-off signs with ease.

You are very happy about your improved vision, and you see yourself smiling with satisfaction.

REFERENCES

Ballard, P., Doerr, H. and Varni, J., Arrest of a Disabling Eye Disorder Using Biofeedback. "Psychophysiology," 1972, 9:271.

Barber, T.X., Implications for Human Capabilities and Potentialities: Improving Nearsighted Vision. "Biofeedback and Self-Control," 1975, 5:60-62.

Carter, D.B., Evaluation of the Placebo Effect in Optometry. "American Journal of Optometry," 1973, 50:94-103.

Corbett, M.D., "Help Yourself to Better Eyesight." North Hollywood: Wilshire Book Co., 1974.

Cornsweet, T.N. and Crane, H.D., Training the Visual Accommodation System. "Vision Research," 1973, 13: 713-715.

Davison, G.C. and Singleton, L.A., A Preliminary Report of Improved Vision Under Hypnosis. "International Journal of Clinical and Experimental Hypnosis," 1967, 15:57-62.

Dorcus, R.M., Modification by Suggestion of Some Vestibular and Visual Responses. "American Journal of Psychology," 1937, 49:82-87.

Eyles, M.A., Some Psycho-Physiological Aspects of Vision Related to Orthoptic Procedure. "British Orthoptic Journal," 1956, 13:7-13.

Forrest, D.W. Von Senden, Mesmer and the Recovery of Sight in the Blind. "American Journal of Psychology," 1974, 87:719-722.

Giddings, J.W., Effect of Reinforcement of Visual Activity in Myopic Adults. "American Journal of Optometry and Physiological Optics," 1974, 51:181-188.

Graham, C. and Leibowitz, H.W., The Effect of Suggestion on Visual Acuity. "International Journal of Clinical and Experimental Hypnosis," 1972, 20:169-186.

Gregory, R.L., "Eye and Brain: The Psychology of Seeing." New York: McGraw Hill, 1973.

Horowitz, M., "Image Formation and Cognition." New York: Appleton, Century, Crofts, 1970.

Lanyon, R.I. and Giddings, J.W., Psychological Approaches to Myopia: A Review. "American Journal of Optometry and Physiological Optics," 1974, 51:271-281.

LeGron, L., Relief of Myopia by Hypnosis and Eye Training. "Diseases of the Nervous System," 1951, 12:142.

Marg, E., An Investigation of Voluntary as Distinguished from Reflex Accommodation. "American Journal of Optometry," 1951, 28:347-356.

Prather, D.C., Differential Reinforcement of the Human Pupillary Response. "Behavioral Science," 1973, 18:420-423.

Provine, R.R. and Enoch, J.M., On Voluntary Ocular Accommodation. "Perception and Psychophysics," 1975, 17:209-212.

Rada, R.T., Visual Conversion Reaction in Children. II. Follow Up. "Psychosomatics," 1973, 14:271-276.

Sells, S.B. and Fixott, R.S., Evaluation of Research on Effects of Visual Training on Visual Functions. "American Journal of Ophthalmology," 1957, 44:230-236.

Sisson, E.D., Voluntary Control of Accommodation. "Journal of General Psychology," 1938, 18:195-198.

Shinkman, P.G., Bruce, C.J. and Pfingst, B.E., Operant Conditioning of Single-Unit Response Patterns in Visual Cortex. "Science," 1974, 184:1194-1196.

Spilker, B., Kamiya, J., Callway, E. and Yeager, C.L., Visual Evoked Responses in Subjects Trained to Control Alpha Rhythms. "Psychophysiology," 1969, 5:683-695.

Theodor, L.H., Hysterical Blindness, a Case Report and Study Using a Modern Psychophysical Technique. "Canadian Journal of Ophthalmology," 1973, 8:353-355.

Yoss, R.E., Moyer, N.M. and Hollenhorst, R.W., Pupil Size and Spontaneous Pupillary Waves Associated With Alertness, Drowsiness, and Sleep. "Neurology," 1970, 20:545-554.

CHAPTER 18:
CONTROLLING A TUMOR WITH TOTAL MIND POWER.

Although proofs of the ability of the mind to control serious tumors are incomplete, those suffering from them have nothing to lose by trying, and there is evidence that even something less potent than Total Mind Power has helped those suffering from tumors.

An example of the mind's ability to influence cancer prognosis comes from the medical field of therapeutic radiology. Several doctors in this field, at medical centers around the country, have divided patients under treatment for cancer into groups. One group receives routine X-ray therapy for the particular type of cancer. The other group, made up of persons suffering from the same type of cancer, receives the same therapy, but is instructed in the use of mental imagery that gives them a more positive outlook about their possibility of recovery.

It has been found in these instances that the groups using imagery and developing more positive attitudes had a better overall prognosis that the groups exposed only to the X-ray treatments. And that was when the group using mental imagery was making use of only conscious thought, the 10 percent of mind power most of us use in our daily lives. How much more effective would the treatment be with the use of Total Mind Power?

Total Mind Power can give you a distinct advantage in the battle to overcome any condition, even one as serious as cancer, especially when its motivating force is added to the discoveries of modern medicine.

Dr. Carl Simonton, a radiation therapist with Oncology Associates, Fort Worth, Texas, uses a combination of meditation, visualization and biofeedback techniques in treating cancer patients.

He believes that using radiation treatment along with the full cooperation and participation of the mind provides better results than using only radiation treatment.

In an interview he says, "Too many patients are getting well to ignore that something different is happening."

The thrust of Total Mind Power is to use it along with the best medical treatments for with its use the patient has nothing to lose and hopefully much to gain.

Before you create a transcript for yourself aimed at a tumor, whether it is as serious as a cancer or a less serious growth, it will be helpful to get as much information as possible from your doctor. He will be able to describe characteristics of the growth that will help you in developing an imaginative and vivid picture.

For instance, suppose you have a wart on your hand. The doctor explains that the little black dots in the center are the blood vessels that nourish it; that it has a nerve supply and is, of course, attached to the skin of your hand.

Now, use your imagination to create a vivid picture for your transcript. Your picture might include a pump with an on/off switch and tubes leading from the pump to the wart. In the off position the switch cuts off the blood supply to the wart. Visualize the nerve supply from the brain being cut off in the same way as the blood supply, if you wish. Picture the effect on the wart as the nourishment stops—it begins to change color, to shrink or dry up, and finally drops away from your hand.

If you are being treated by a doctor for the wart, incorporate the treatment in your transcript. If, for instance, he has you apply a brown medicine, direct your mind to see it penetrating the wart, killing the cells inside it, so that in combination with the cutting off of nourishment from blood and nerves, it causes the wart to dry up and drop away.

Total Mind Power methods also may be applied to more serious problems, such as a malignant tumor of the lung. Here, too, endeavor to get from your doctor a fundamental understanding of the details of the growth, so you can create mind pictures appropriate to it.

Here is a brief example of a transcript form to guide one suffering from this form of cancer in creating an individual recording. The person will expand on the details, incorporating, as always, the maximum number of sensory impressions:

You visualize as much about the problem as possible.

You see that the tumor has a nerve supply that you can cut off by a switch in your head.

You see the tumor shriveling.

In your mind,

you see this process taking place.

You now direct your mind to send out antibodies to fight the tumor cells.

You see in your mind's eye an antibody-making machine in your body.

You instruct the machine,
when turned "on,"
to release antibodies that go to the tumor and attack the growth.

You could picture the "antibody" machine releasing tiny, animal-like creatures that literally gobble up the tumor cells, or amoeba-like organisms that engulf and digest them.

In the case of a serious condition such as this, it is a good idea to use the Total Mind Power techniques once or twice a day indefinitely.

Total Mind Power is not suggested as a substitute for medical help or as a cure. Its use can do no harm, will almost certainly do some good, and can in any event relieve pain, as described in the chapter on pain.

REFERENCES

Ader, R. and Cohen, N., Behaviorally Conditioned Immuno-Suppression. "Psychosomatic Medicine," 1975, 37:333-340.

Allington, H.V., Review of the Psychotherapy of Warts. "Archives of Dermatology and Syphilology," 1952, 66: 316-326.

August, R.V., Hypnotic Induction of Hypothermia: An Additional Approach to Post Operative Control of Cancer Recurrence. "The American Journal of Clinical Hypnosis," 1975, 18:52-55.

Belli, J.A., Proliferation Kinetics of Normal and Tumor Cells. Factors Which Influence Radiotherapeutic Response. "Radiology," 1972, 105:143-149.

Benk, H.A.V., Moore, V., Sharpington, C. and Orton, C., Production of Metastases by a Primary Tumor Irradiated Under Aerobic and Anaerobic Conditions in Vivo. "British Journal of Cancer," 1972, 26:402-412.

Bolen, J.S., Meditation and Psychotherapy in the Treatment of Cancer. "Psychic Magazine, August 1973, 19-22.

Bradley, R.A. (ed.), The Varieties of Healing Experiences: Exploring Psychic Phenomena in Healing. "The Academy of Parapsychology and Medicine," October 1971.

Clawson, T.A. and Swade, R.H., The Hypnotic Control of Blood Flow and Pain: The Cure of Warts and the Potential for the Use of Hypnosis in the Treatment of Cancer. "The American Journal of Clinical Hypnosis," 1975, 17:160-169.

Ewin, D.M., Condyloma Acuminatum: Successful Treatment of Four Cases by Hypnosis. "The American Journal of Clinical Hypnosis," 1974, 17:73-78.

Frank, J.D., "Persuasion and Healing." New York: Schocken Books, 1963.

Friedman-Kien, A., Virus Infections-Warts. D.J. Demis, R.G. Crounse, R.L. Dobson and J. McGuire (eds.), "Clinical Dermatology." New York: Harper and Row, Publishers, 1972, Unit 14-14, 3:1-10.

Frohlich, E.D. (ed.), "Pathophysiology: Altered Regulatory Mechanisms in Disease." Philadelphia: J.B. Lippincott Company, 1972.

Green, E., Green, A. and Walters, D., Voluntary Control of Internal States: Psychological and Physiological. "Journal of Transpersonal Psychology," 1970, 1:1-26.

Kopf, A., Tumors of Epidermal and Follicular Origin—Keratoacnthoma. D.J. Demis, R.G. Crounse, R.L. Dobson and J. McGuire (eds.), "Clinical Dermatology." New York: Harper and Row, Publishers, 1972, Unit 21-9, 4:1-7.

LaBaw, W., Holton, C., Tewell, K. and Eccles, D., The Use of Self-Hypnosis by Children with Cancer. "The American Journal of Clinical Hypnosis," 1975, 17:233-238.

Miller, N., Learning of Glandular and Visceral Responses. "Current Status of Physiological Psychology," 1972.

Sacerdote, P., Theory and Practice of Pain Control in Malignancy and Other Protracted or Recurring Painful Illnesses. "International Journal of Clinical and Experimental Hypnosis," 1970, 18:160-180.

Schmale, A.H. and Iker, P., The Effect of Hopelessness and the Development of Cancer. "Psychosomatic Medicine," 1966, 28:714-721.

Sinclair-Gieben, A.H.C. and Chalmers, D., Evaluation of Treatment of Warts by Suggestion. "Lancet," 1959, 2:480.

Snyder, C. and Noble, M., Operant Conditioning of Vasoconstriction. "Journal of Experimental Psychology," 1968, 77:263-268.

Solomon, G.F., Amkrant, A.A. and Kasper, P., Immunity, Emotions and Stress, "Psychotherapeutic Psychosomatics," 1974, 23:209-217.

Sullivan, G.B., The Role of the Mind in Cancer. "San Francisco Examiner and Chronicle, November 9, 1975.

Surman, O.S., Gottlief, S.K. and Hackett, T.P., Hypnotic Treatment of a Child With Warts. "American Journal of Clinical Hypnosis," 1972, 15:12-14.

Surman, O.S., Gottlief, S.K., Hackett, T.P. and Silverberg, E.L., Hypnosis in the Treatment of Warts. "Archives of General Psychiatry," 1973, 28:439-441.

Taylor, G.J., Letter: Psychological Factors in Cancer. "Canadian Psychiatric Association Journal," 1974, 19:421.

Ullman, M., On the Psyche and Warts: Suggestion and Warts: A Review and Comment. "Psychosomatic Medicine," 1959, 21:473-488.

Witten, V.H. and Zak, F.G., Multiple Primary Self-Healing Prickle-Cell Epithelioma of the Skin, "Cancer," 1952, 5:539.

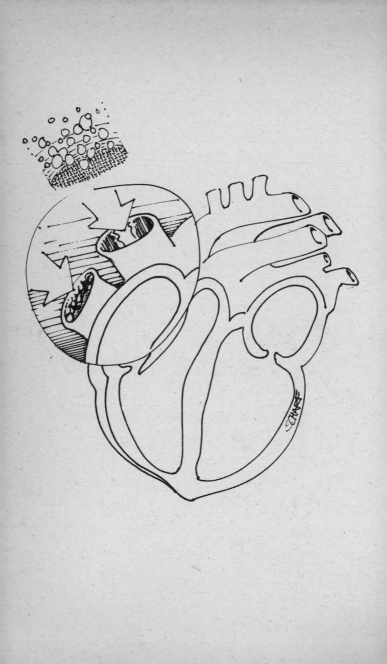

CHAPTER 19:
HOW TO DECREASE THE POSSIBILITY OF A
HEART ATTACK WITH TOTAL MIND POWER.

Among the diseases that may develop over a period
of years without noticeable symptoms is coronary
heart disease. Most tests do not show when an other-
wise normally healthy person is building up fatty deposits in his coronary arteries. There are sophisticated tests to show the status of the person with
advanced heart disease, but they are inadequate for
revealing the potential heart problems of the seeming-
ly healthy, and so many persons never know they are
in trouble until a heart attack occurs.

Even those whose condition has been diagnosed,
and who are being treated, run risks.

When I was a resident in internal medicine, one
of the things that impressed me greatly was the risks
many patients under treatment for heart disease and
related problems were running because of the drugs
used to control their problems. Too often I saw
patients die from drug-related complications such as
abnormal rates and patterns of heartbeat.

Some of the medications are tricky to use, and
the patient receiving them must be watched carefully.

I remember an elderly man who took an overdose of his digitalis. He was brought into the Emergency Room in a dying condition and by the time his problem had been diagnosed, it was too late to save him. The overdose had caused an abnormal heart rate that was difficult to distinguish from an abnormal rate caused by a heart attack, and the treatment for the two is different.

Later I had occasion to talk with members of his family. They told me he was taking several medications, and his eyesight was poor, so he had probably taken the wrong pills, and thus an overdose of the digitalis when he thought he was taking something else.

The difficulty of diagnosing many heart problems, the risky nature of some of the medications, and the fact that an astonishingly high rate of patients simply don't follow their doctors' directions, make it extra important that there be some way to prevent and alleviate heart conditions.

Studies throughout the world have shown that the mind *can* influence the normal heart rate as well as abnormal heart rate patterns, and can lower high blood pressure that is a factor in some heart attacks. Thus the healthy individual can use his mind to remain that way, and the heart patient can easily and conveniently apply Total Mind Power techniques, along with his doctor's treatment, to influence the course of his illness. And Total Mind Power can always be used to alleviate pain.

Men and women with heart conditions or vulnerable by reason of heredity or other factors such as "sugar diabetes," would be well advised to plan daily Total Mind Power sessions. The following transcript is a guide for them in preparing one that meets their needs:

You see in your mind a picture of your heart.

You see your heart muscles being fed by your coronary arteries.

You may visualize this as an engine receiving gasoline through a fuel line, or in any other graphic way you please.

You remember that a heart attack occurs when these coronary blood vessels narrow, or are plugged up by fat deposits.

You direct your mind to keep these particular blood vessels free of fatty deposits, so they'll remain open and clear all your life.

You now direct your mind to send out a chemical to dissolve any fat deposits that may have already formed.

You also direct your mind to send impulses to your heart to keep it beating at its normal rhythm, no matter how much strain you might be under.

You feel the beat of your heart, and with each beat you direct your mind to make your heart stronger.

You also increase the blood supply to your heart by making more blood vessels bring it nourishment.

You know that these extra blood vessels to your heart are important in case certain vessels become plugged up.

The relaxation and general benefits you get from
the use of Total Mind Power take enormous stress off
of your heart,
and you develop a great sense of confidence in your
ability to prevent heart disease.

Now you hear the normal beating of your heart
as it changes rhythm with each breath you take.

You know that this change of rhythm is normal,
but any other changes that might occur—such as very
irregular beats—are quickly changed back to normal
beats by your mind.

It does this by sending directions to your heart
by way of the nerves from your brain.

You are very happy to think of your ability to
prevent heart problems.

For example,
you can direct your mind to filter out excess
cholesterol by use of a special screen that you imagine
in one of the main blood vessels going to your heart.

You may see the blood vessels as tubes or pipes
leading into your heart,
and you see a regulating switch in your mind that
controls the amount of blood feeding your heart.
Whenever the blood supply declines,
you turn on this switch,
and more nourishing blood is instantly sent to
your heart.

You see a special signal light go on in your brain
if any drugs or chemicals enter your system that might
interfere with your heart rate,
or with the blood supply to your heart.
Whenever this light goes on,
you direct your mind to send out special chemicals
from your liver to attack these foreign substances.

You direct your mind to control the pressure of
the blood that flows to your heart.
This makes the pressure in your blood vessels
normal.
You can see your doctor taking your blood
pressure and congratulating you on its normality.
You take great pride in your ability to control
these functions of your body,
and you develop a sense of security about your life.

The precise nature of your heart condition will dictate the contents of the transcript you create. If angina pectoris (chest pain associated with coronary heart disease) is the problem, you could easily combine the directions for relieving pain with the ones intended to thwart heart attacks. There are countless other combinations possible.

Reminder: No matter how effective Total Mind Power may be in practice, it is *not* meant to take the place of conventional medical treatment. It is to be used *in addition* to the care provided by your doctor.

REFERENCES

Bergman, J.S. and Johnson, H.J., Sources of Information Which Affect Training and Raising of Heart Rate. "Psychophysiology," 1972, 9:30-39.

Blanchard, E.B., Young, L.D. and McLeod, P., Awareness of Heart Activity and Self-Control of Heart Rate. "Psychophysiology," 1972, 9:63-68.

Bleeker, E.R. and Engel, B.T., Learned Control of Cardiac Rate and Cardiac Conduction in the Wolff-Parkinson-White Syndrome. "New England Journal of Medicine," 1973, 288:560-562.

Bleeker, E.R. and Engel, B.T., Learned Control of Ventricular Rate in Patients With Atrial Fibrillation. "Psychosomatic Medicine," 1973, 35:161-175.

Brener, J., Factors Influencing the Specificity of Voluntary Cardiovascular Control. "Biofeedback and Self-Control," 1974, 5:147-180.

Brener, J., Learned Control of Cardiovascular Processes: Feedback Mechanisms and Therapeutic Applications. K.S. Calhoun, H.E. Adams and K.M. Mitchell (eds.), "Innovative Treatment Methods in Psychopathology." New York: John Wiley and Sons, Inc., 1974a, 245-272.

Campos, J.J. and Johnson, H.J., The Effects of Verbalization Instructions and Visual Attention on Heart Rate and Skin Conductance. "Psychophysiology," 1966, 2:305.

Frederick, A.N.D. and Barber, T.X., Yoga, Hypnosis, and Self-Control of Cardiovascular Functions. "Proceedings, 80th Annual Convention, American Psychological Association, 1972, 859-860.

French, J.R.P. and Caplan, R.D., Psycho-Social Factors in Coronary Heart Disease. "Industrial Medicine," 1970, 39:383-401.

Friedman, M. and Rosenman, R.H., "Type A Behavior and Your Heart." New York: Knopf, 1974.

Engel, B.T. and Chism, R.A., Operant Conditioning of Heart Rate Speeding. "Psychophysiology," 1967a, 3:418-426.

Engel, B.T. and Hansen, S.P., Operant Conditioning of Rate Slowing. "Psychophysiology," 1966, 3:176-187.

Gruen, W.A., A Successful Application of Systematic Self-Relaxation and Self-Suggestions About Post-Operative Reactions in a Case of Cardiac Surgery. "International Journal of Clinical and Experimental Hypnosis," 1972, 20:143-151.

Headrick, M.W., Feather, B.W. and Wells, D.T., Unidirectional and Large Magnitude Heart Rate Changes With Augmented Sensory Feedback. "Psychophysiology," 1971, 8:132-142.

Hnatiow, M. and Lang, B.J., Learned Stabilization of Cardiac Rate. "Psychophysiology," 1965, 1:330-336.

Rosenman, R.H., Emotional Factors in Coronary Heart Disease. "Postgraduate Medicine," 1967, 42:164-171.

Schapiro, D., Schwartz, G.E. and Benson, H., Biofeedback: A Behavioral Approach to Cardiovascular Self-Control. "Contemporary Problems in Cardiology," 1974, 1:279-292.

Schwartz, G.E., Cardiac Responses to Self-Induced Thoughts. "Psychophysiology," 1971, 8:462-467.

Scott, R.W., et al, The Use of Shaping and Reinforcement in the Operant Acceleration and Deceleration of Heart Rate. "Behaviour Research and Therapy," 1973, 11:179-185.

Spence, D.P., Lugo, M. and Youdin, R., Cardiac Change as a Function of Attention to and Awareness of Continuous Verbal Text. "Science," 1972, 176:1344-1346.

Stephens, J.H., Harris, A.H. and Brady, J.V., Large Magnitude Heart Rate Changes in Subjects Instructed to Change Their Heart Rates and Given Interoceptive Feedback. "Psychophysiology," 1972, 9:283-285.

Stephens, J.H., Harris, A.H., Brady, J.V. and Shaffer, J.W., Psychological and Physiological Variables Associated with Large Magnitude Voluntary Heart Rate Changes. "Psychophysiology," 1975, 12:381-387.

Bell, I.R. and Schwartz, G.E., Voluntary Control and Reactivity of Human Heart Rate. "Psychophysiology," 1975, 12:339-348.

CHAPTER 20:
TOTAL MIND POWER FOR SLOWING DOWN
THE AGING PROCESS.

Have you observed that some people look better than others, even though they are the same age? For some it is a natural occurrence that most likely cannot be controlled, but for many, getting older does not necessarily mean rapid deterioration.

I recall a business executive, Stewart, who came to my office complaining of feeling unusually tired. He also expressed concern about his pale and sallow look, which made him appear much older than his 52 years. Obviously he was tense and depressed.

A complete examination, including chest X-rays, blood and urine tests, showed no physical reasons for his problems.

I asked him if he had ever thought of using his mind to influence his general health. He said no, that he believed his problems were due to the general deterioration that goes with the inevitable process of aging and that nothing could be done.

I suggested several Total Mind Power techniques to him. A week later he returned to my office, his entire appearance dramatically altered. He was vibrant, the color and tone of his skin were almost youthful, and he showed no signs of depression.

It is estimated that the illnesses of over 80 percent of the patients who visit private physicians are psychosomatic (caused by the patient's mental attitude). These illnesses include stomach ulcers, constant headaches, muscular weakness and myriad other complaints. Millions of dollars are spent every year by persons seeking cures for problems that originate in their minds.

If the mind can cause an illness, it seems only natural that it can cure that illness. Sadly, such thinking has not been accepted by the public nor by many practicing physicians. In defense of the physicians, it must be acknowledged that most are so busy attending to their patients and relieving symptoms that they do not have the time to spend instructing them in how to use their minds to remove the causes.

Scientists involved in studying the aging process claim it would not be unreasonable for the human life span to average 120 to 150 years. They believe that modern man, especially in the Western world, dies prematurely.

In support of this theory, there is evidence that people of ancient times did live longer than we do, just as isolated groups today have been discovered who live far longer.

Aging can be classified as a disease, many of the symptoms of which appear to be psychosomatic in origin, but nonetheless uncomfortable, even fatal. The pressures and anxieties of our modern environment seem to accelerate the aging process, a problem our distant ancestors apparently did not have to face.

Hereditary factors, too, influence aging. Some inherit stronger constitutions than others and so are better able to resist disease and pressure. But history is full of examples of persons who led long and highly productive lives in spite of chronic illness and frailty. These persons seem to have used the power of their minds to overcome their physical weaknesses.

If you wish to do the same, make your transcript and start growing younger.

The Step Two transcript you create for slowing down the aging process should be as colorful and imaginative as you can possibly make it and should include these basic elements:

1. Visualize yourself continuing to live your life in a youthful and vigorous fashion indefinitely.

2. Direct your mind to produce the specific effects you want. For instance, if you do not want to look old and wrinkled, see yourself with smooth, supple, wrinkle-free skin.

3. Picture yourself as extremely alert and athletic, moving freely and easily as you did when you were a teenager.

4. If certain ailments have accompanied the aging process, incorporate specific transcripts to deal with those problems as well as with aging.

5. Call forth all of your senses. Direct your mind to improve your sense of taste, since it and the other senses are reputed to become less sensitive as you age. Direct your mind to make your hearing more acute, to heighten your senses of smell, touch and sight.

6. Visualize any aches and pains you have accepted as inevitable as floating away forever.

Step Three repetitions should be at least once a week for an indefinite period, since your objective is to preserve your body by using your mind, and this is really a lifetime program.

Do not be disturbed if some people do not accept Total Mind Power as a practical force. It is natural, harmless, and in no way conflicts with any treatment. They should, at least, be delighted that your mental attitude is good, as it surely will be. You can rest assured that Total Mind Power can bring you nothing but good. The feeling of well-being it gives is in itself an important aid to slowing the aging process. Overcoming anxiety and tension contributes markedly to a feeling of youthfulness.

The sums of money spent on cosmetics, plastic surgery, contraptions intended to retard the aging process, the emphasis in advertising on youth, prove that we are highly motivated to retain youth and vigor and will try almost anything that promises results. Total Mind Power provides the simplest, least expensive and most convenient way to win the struggle against age.

REFERENCES

Barber, T.X., Implications for Human Capabilities and Potentialities: Control of Skin Temperature. "Biofeedback and Self Control 1974," 1975, 5:58-60.

Beary, J.F., A Simple Psychophysiologic Technique Which Elicits the Hypometabolic Changes of the Relaxation Response. "Psychosomatic Medicine," 1974, 36:115-120.

Belluci, G., Feedback Effects on the Performance and Self-Reinforcing Behavior of Elderly and Young Adult Women. "Journal of Gerontology," 1975, 30:456-460.

Brown, B., "New Mind, New Body." New York: Harper and Row, Publishers, 1974.

Fischer, H.K. and Dlin, B.M., Man's Determination of His Time of Illness or Death. "Geriatrics," 1971, 26:89-94.

Green, E.E., Green, A.M. and Walters, E.D., Self-Regulation of Internal States. "Progress of Cybernetics: Proceedings of the International Congress of Cybernetics." London: Gordon and Breach, 1970, 1299-1317.

Hughes, W.G. and Shean, G.D., Personality and Ability to Control the Galvanic Skin Response. "Psychophysiology," 1971, 8:247.

Kugler, H.J., "Slowing Down the Aging Process." New York: Pyramid Books, 1973.

Lazarus, R.S., "Psychological Stress and the Coping Process." New York: McGraw-Hill, 1966.

Samuels, M. and Bennett, H., "Be Well." New York: Random House-Book Works, 1974.

Schultz, J.H. and Luthe, W., "Autogenic Therapy." New York: Grune and Stratton, 1969.

Selye, H., "Stress Without Distress." Philadelphia: J.B. Lippincott, 1974.

Selye, H., "The Stress of Life." New York: McGraw-Hill, 1956.

Venables, P.H. and Martin, I., "A Manual of Psychophysiological Methods," Amsterdam: North-Holland Publishing, 1967.

Wallace, R.K. and Wilson, A.F., A Wakeful Hypometabolic State. "American Journal of Physiology," 1971.

Wells, D.T., Feather, B.W. and Headrick, M.W., The Effects of Immediate Feedback Upon Voluntary Control of Salivary Rate. "Psychophysiology," 1973, 10:501-509.

CHAPTER 21:
CONTROLLING OTHER DISEASES WITH
TOTAL MIND POWER

Severe warts in a sensitive area were troublesome to Jane, a girl in her late teens who came to my office one day. She told me the warts had been treated chemically several times and removed surgically, but they kept returning. Jane said that because the treatments were so painful she had considered suicide.

Realizing her warts were due to a viral infection and could return despite any treatment, I asked Jane if she would agree to use Total Mind Power techniques before trying any further medical applications. Jane agreed, applied Total Mind Power, and within two weeks her warts had disappeared.

Warts often do disappear spontaneously, or as a result of treatments whose efficacy it is difficult to explain. The mind's influence on a tumor growth of this type may be due to a stepping up of some immunological resistance to the wart virus, or to a mental control of the blood supply to the area. Directions for the transcript for this patient were aimed along this line.

As long as you have some knowledge of the cause or action of a disease, you can create visualizations for transcripts aimed at its alleviation or cure.

Total Mind Power advocates the use of the mind to enhance medical treatment in the healing process.

In an interview Dr. Kenneth R. Pelletier, research psychologist at the Langley Porter Neuropsychiatric Institute and director of the Psychosomatic Institute Center at Gladman, California, said, "Once an individual adopts the concept that he is an active and responsible participant in the process of self-healing, then he is no longer the passive victim of a disease.

"In this manner, the creative capacity of the patient is engaged in the therapeutic process and new possibilities and approaches become possible when people learn how to draw upon their own inner resources."

For example, if an individual suffers from Diabetes Mellitus (commonly known as sugar diabetes), a physician might explain the cause in layman's terms as faulty utilization of sugar taken into the body due to a lack of naturally produced insulin from the pancreas. Although medically oversimplified, this explanation provides adequate material for making mind pictures to be used in a transcript.

Total Mind Power might be applied by imagining abundant insulin flowing from the pancreas in a flood to meet an influx of rock candy. At the same time, the individual might direct the mind to metabolize the sugars and starches eaten, more efficiently.

Total Mind Power also could be used to overcome any temptation to cheat by eating forbidden foods, such as those high in sugars and starches.

This triple attack through the hitherto unused

powers of the mind would very likely soon lead to a reduction in the insulin dosage prescribed by your physician.

Total Mind Power is not based upon faith healing or any religious concept. It is not dependent upon strengthening your will power or powers of concentration. It is based on scientific procedures and techniques and it will work when used as described in these pages, whether you believe in it or are only trying it as a last resort.

If you are faced with a difficult problem, be it academic, emotional, psychological or physical, you probably have sufficient motivation to try Total Mind Power now. Regardless of what your problem is, these techniques will help you.

REFERENCES

Franks, J.D., "Persuasion and Healing." Baltimore: The Johns Hopkins Press, 1961.

Johnson, R.F.Q. and Barber, T.X., "Hypnotic and Non-Hypnotic Suggestions for Wart Removal: An Empirical Exploration." Medfield, Mass.: Medfield Foundation, 1976.

Glueck, B.C. and Stroebel, C.F., Biofeedback and Meditation in the Treatment of Psychiatric Illnesses. "Comprehensive Psychiatry," 1975, 16:303-321.

Graham, D.T., Kabler, J.D. and Graham, F.K., Physiological Responses to the Suggestions of Attitudes Specific for Hives and Hypertension. "Psychosomatic Medicine," 1962, 24:159-169.

McDowell, M. Hypnosis in Dermatology. In J.M. Schneck (ed.), "Hypnosis In Modern Medicine," (2nd ed.) Springfield, Ill.: Charles C. Thomas, 1959, 101-115.

Philipp, R.L., Suggestion and Relaxation in Asthmatics. "Journal of Psychosomatic Research," 1971, 16:193-204.

Sullivan, G.B., The Role of the Mind in Cancer. "The San Francisco Examiner and Chronicle," November 9, 1975.

CHAPTER 22:
STOPPING FEARS AND PHOBIAS WITH TOTAL MIND POWER.

Everyone has some fears and phobias, and most of them exert minimal influence on our lives, but now and then one crops up that makes life uncomfortable, or may even interfere seriously with social life or business progress. Then it becomes necessary to do something about it.

If elevators terrify you, you must either cure the fear or get into condition for climbing mountains of stairs. If flying is your special hangup, you will have to overcome the fear or reconcile yourself to ground travel.

Total Mind Power can help you overcome any fear or phobia that you wish to overcome.

One day a friend admitted to a tremendous fear of airplanes and of flying. This was doubly unfortunate, because his business required that he fly often.

John couldn't account for the fear, and he had even been to a psychiatrist in an effort to solve his problem. And he did much soul searching and self-analysis, but his fear increased. Merely understanding the fear did not dispel it. He was particularly concerned about his problem, because he was definitely going to lose his job if he did not solve it.

I told John that recognizing a problem was not an automatic cure, but that Total Mind Power techniques would work for him.

He tried them, and within a week had overcome his fear. He has been flying for several years since then and says he has no emotional or psychological problems now.

I asked him what he had put into his transcript.

He said that for Step One he had adapted the balloon journey transcript in Chapter 7 to his needs, shortening it a bit because of his limited time. He usually played it early in the morning, because that was more convenient for him than at night, although occasionally he did use it just before going to bed. That is one of the prime advantages of Total Mind Power techniques—they are adaptable to every individual's needs and preferences.

For Step Number Two he developed a transcript in which he saw himself piloting a glider and being towed to a great height. He would feel the buoyancy as the glider flew on the wind currents. He would taste and smell the clean, fresh air and hear the whoosh of the wings as they cut through the air.

He also incorporated in his transcript many feelings, such as how elated he would feel whenever he made a beautiful, gliding turn and how excited he was over the beauty of the earth beneath him.

He described how he developed an enjoyment of flying and how his fears drifted away like the clouds he visualized floating by him on his gliding flights.

For Step Three he repeated the transcripts daily for a week, then every other day for the second week, although by then he had lost his fear of flying.

After that he would use his transcript about every three months to experience the exhilaration of gliding in the air, even though he had not developed any new fears.

Total Mind Power helps you overcome fear, whatever the cause and whatever the subject.

If you have a phobia about going to the dentist because of fear of pain, you might not only work out a transcript for making yourself comfortable about going to the dentist, but work on a transcript designed to eliminate any possible pain (as described in the chapter on pain).

Once you have tried it, you will find life has extra savor when you are freed from the limitations of unreasoning fears. You will experience a special sense of exhilaration as you realize you are no longer afraid, and in addition, you have right at hand a weapon against any future fears that may arise.

REFERENCES

Borkovec, T.D., The Effects of Instructional Suggestion and Physiological Cues on Analogue Fear. "Behavior Therapy," 1973a, 4:185-192.

Friedman, D.E. and Silverstone, J.T., Treatment of Phobic Patients by Systematic Desensitization. "Lancet," 1967, 1:470.

Grings, W.W. and Uno, T., Counter Conditioning: Fear and Relaxation. "Psychophysiology," 1968, 4:479-485.

Gurman, A.S., Treatment of a Case of Public-Speaking Anxiety by In-Vivo Desensitization and Cue-Controlled Relaxation. "Journal of Behavior Therapy and Experimental Psychiatry," 1973, 4:51-54.

Lang, P.J., Melamed, B.G. and Hart, J., A Psychophysiological Analysis of Fear Modification Using an Automated Desensitization Procedure. "Journal of Abnormal Psychology," 1970, 76:221.

Marks, I., The Origins of Phobic States. "American Journal of Psychotherapy," 1970, 24:652-676.

CHAPTER 23:
USING TOTAL MIND POWER TO OVERCOME
ALCOHOL AND DRUGS.

Alcoholism and drug addiction are problems of increasing concern in our society, and their cure by conventional means is one of the most difficult. Total Mind Power can accomplish that cure, releasing the victim from a terrifying burden.

The vast majority of persons suffering from the effects of overuse of drugs or of alcohol (which is really a drug) know the dangers of their habit, but simply cannot overcome it.

Whether the drug is a simple one like aspirin or a dangerous one such as morphine, whether alcohol or sleeping pills are your downfall, you can free yourself from the habit that is damaging your health and interfering with your pursuit of a happy and successful life.

The question of when or if you need treatment can be decided only by you. The threshold of danger differs for every individual, and even differs for one individual at different times. What is a dangerously large quantity for one person may be only a moderate intake for another. Medical advice and literature on the subject of addiction may be helpful, but in the last analysis only you can judge what treatment. and how extensive a treatment, you need. You alone know for sure whether or not a drug or a drink is incapacitating you, affecting your health, spoiling your relationships with other people.

Step Three of the Total Mind Power techniques, the reinforcement, varies with each individual also. If you are heavily addicted to a drug or alcohol you will need frequent, perhaps daily, sessions for an indefinite period. The occasional drinker who merely wants to cut down his drinking may need only infrequent applications of the techniques.

Applied frequently enough, Total Mind Power techniques will relieve even the most serious habit.

The following model transcript for overcoming excessive use of alcohol may be used as it is or altered to suit your special needs, and it may be changed around in appropriate fashion to apply to a drug habit:

You imagine yourself thinking about your favorite alcoholic beverage and you can clearly visualize the drink.

You know that you would like to decrease your use of alcohol because of all the problems it creates for you and those around you.

You direct your mind to give you control over your drinking.

You picture a switch in your mind that controls

your desire for alcohol.

When the switch is turned off,
you lose your taste for alcohol.

Now you can see your alcoholic drink even
more clearly,
but you're amazed to find that you have lost your
taste for the drink.

In fact,
you see that you have lost interest in all alcohol,
and you develop a great deal of satisfaction in your
ability to control your desire for drinking.

You begin to think of other drinks that are nonalcoholic,
and you begin to develop a taste for them.

One of these might be aromatic organic tea
served with honey.

You see yourself in a party situation where a
drink is being offered to you,
and you picture yourself turning it down.

You instead request a soda with an olive
or lime,
or a similar refreshing drink.

You start to develop an even stronger taste
for nonalcoholic beverages that are usually available

in the same places and situations where liquor is offered.

Some of these drinks are grapefruit and orange juice,

or any other nonalcholic drinks you prefer.

You remember all of the bad sensations and feelings that alcohol always gives you,

especially the day after you drink.

These memories become extremely vivid whenever an opportunity for drinking alcohol comes up.

You notice that if you have a craving for alcohol at any time,

you can replace this urge with a desire for food.

You see yourself in another situation where you are considering taking an alcoholic drink,

but suddenly you lose the desire for the drink and think of your favorite food.

You smell and taste this dish and you see yourself eating it heartily.

Any time you are in such a situation you see yourself going out of your way to eat something as soon as possible to lessen your desire for alcohol.

After you have eaten you notice that any thoughts of alcohol you may have had are completely out of place with your tastes.

You take great pleasure in the foods that replace
your thoughts about alcohol,
and you develop a sense of accomplishment.

You can feel your body becoming healthier
as you begin each new day without drinking,
and you feel a tremendous well-being that you
want to maintain for the rest of your life.

You find that you can go to sleep far more
easily,
and that your dreams are beautiful.

Since you can sleep better,
you experience a feeling of strength and vitality
when you wake up in the morning.

All of the relationships in your life improve.

You decide for yourself that all of these improvements give you so much more pleasure than drinking,
you want to cast aside the use of alcohol.

You have a sense of direction and purpose in
your life that replaces the down feelings you
experienced when you were drinking.

REFERENCES

Baker, T.B., et al, The Effects of Video-Taped Modeling and Self-Confrontation on the Drinking Behavior of Alcoholics. "International Journal of Addiction," 1975, 10:779-793.

Barber, T.X., "LSD, Marihuana, Yoga and Hypnosis." Chicago: Aldine Publishing Co., 1970.

Battozzi, A.A. and Luce, G., Physiological Effects of Meditation Technique and Suggestion for Drug Abuse. "Mental Health Reports-5," Department of Health Education and Welfare, December 1971.

Benson, H., Decreased Alcohol Intake Associated With the Practice of Meditation: A Retrospective Investigation. "Annals of the New York Academy of Science," 1974 233:174-177.

Benson, H., Yoga for Drug Abuse. "New England Journal of Medicine," 1969, 281:11-33.

Blake, B.G., The Application of Behavior Therapy to the Treatment of Alcoholism. "Behavior Research and Therapy," 1965, 3:75-85.

Blake, B.G., A Follow-Up of Alcoholics Treated by Behavior Therapy. "Behavior Research and Therapy," 1967, 5:89-94.

Brecher, E.M., "Licit and Illicit Drugs." New York: Consumers Union, 1971.

Byers, A.P., Training and use of Technicians in the Treatment of Alcoholism With Hypnosis. "The American Journal of Clinical Hypnosis," 1975, 18:90-93.

Fort, J., "Alcohol: Our Greatest Drug Problem." New York: McGraw-Hill Book Company, 1973.

Gattozzi, A.A. and Luce, G.G., Physiological Effects of a Meditation Technique and a Suggestion for Curbing Drug Abuse. "No. HMS 72-9042," Department of Health Education and Welfare, 1971.

Goldiamond, I., Self-Control Procedures in Personal Behavior Problems. "Psychological Reports," 1965, 17:851.

Hamburg, S., Behavior Therapy in Alcoholism. A Critical Review of Broad-Spectrum Approaches. "Journal of Studies on Alcohol," 1975, 36:69-87.

Hartman, C.H., Group Relaxation Training for Control of Impulsive Behavior in Alcoholics. "Behavior Therapy," 1973, 4:173-174.

Jones, B.M. and Parsons, O.A., Alcohol and Consciousness: Getting High and Coming Down. "Psychology Today," January, 1975, 53-58.

Marzetta, B.R., Benson, H. and Wallace, R.K., Combating Drug Dependency in Young People: A New Approach. "Medical Counterpoint," September, 1972, 32-36.

Shafil, M., Meditation and the Prevention of Alcohol Abuse. "American Journal of Psychiatry," 1975, 132:942-945.

CHAPTER 24:
HOW TO INCREASE SEXUAL RESPONSIVENESS
WITH TOTAL MIND POWER.

Sex-related problems are among the most common,
and often seem the most difficult to solve. Two major
difficulties are impotence in the male and the inability
of the female to achieve orgasm. In some instances a
physical deficiency or ailment may be responsible, but
in the majority of cases the cause appears to be psychological.

Sex research centers, clinics and counseling groups
are emerging in response to people's need for help with
these sexual problems, but cures seem few.

Several years ago Jim, who was 30 and had been
to several such clinics came to me, filled with anxieties
and completely confused by the different recommen-
dations for treatment. He had been analyzed and
shown many facets of his problem, but nothing had
helped.

Realizing that whatever the cause of his problem
the most important thing at the moment was the meeting of his basic needs, I described Total Mind Power

techniques and suggested he apply them in his own way.

A week later Jim came to see me again, tremendously excited because not only had his impotence been cured, but Total Mind Power was helping him to become more and more fulfilled.

And then later, I ran into the same man again. He reported that he was very happy, was married, had a child and had no problems related to sex.

Other patients unable to achieve orgasm, to whom I have suggested Total Mind Power as an aid, have had similar experiences. All have expressed gratitude for the discovery that they could use their own minds to solve their problems.

Research studies show that the mind has a tremendous influence over sexual response, so there is ample support for the assurance that you can use your mind to find a richer life for yourself.

If you feel a need for increased sexual response, proceed through Step One—the balloon trip would be good here, and then use for Step Two a transcript that covers the problems you are having in every detail. Your directions should describe and picture exactly what you would like to accomplish. Include all of the emotional and sensory directions possible.

The following transcript applies Toral Mind Power to increasing overall sexual responsiveness:

You see yourself in a lovely castle with someone you love very much.

The two of you are walking through the castle enjoying all of the sights and sounds of the charming scene around you.

Your partner looks so attractive that you suddenly

feel a strong sexual urge come over you.

You begin to speak of romance.

You look into each other's eyes,
and you both desire to be alone with each other.

Both of you can feel a surging impulse in your
bodies.

You are sexually attracted to one another in
the most powerful imaginable way.

You walk faster in search of an isolated room
where you will find privacy with your lover.

You come to a hallway that leads to a flight
of steps.

As you climb the steps,
you can feel and hear your heart beating faster.

You both anticipate the electric moment of
your first embrace.

There's a tall wooden door at the end of the
stairway.

You slowly push it open,
and you both see a large bed in the center of the
room.

A ray of sunlight comes through a beautiful
window and bathes the bed in a lovely glow.

At one side of the room you see a large
wooden tub.

Since you both have been walking in the dusty
courtyard of the castle,
you take off each other's clothes so you may take
a very wonderful,
sensuous bath together.

The bath water is warm and fragrant.

As you wash each other a tingling sensation
comes over your bodies,
and you become sexually aroused.

You touch each other over every part of
your bodies,
and you feel a tremendous sense of exhilaration.

You can sense the thrill building up between you,
and you can feel the expectation of making love.

You begin kissing passionately.

A sweet taste in your mouth seems to signal
that you are ready to unite with one another.

Intoxicating,
aromatic odors pervade the air,
and you can hear soft music coming from a distance.

You both know that you are alone in this
remote paradise.

After you step out of the bath,

you begin to dry each other with large,
soft towels.

Each time you touch,
more excitement builds up,
and you can scarcely wait to be in each other's arms.

You both reach a peak of desire and fall into
the beautiful bed together.

Passion surges over you like an overpowering
wave as you continue to touch and caress.

You begin to massage each other and,
with each touch,
you become more and more excited.

Now you begin stroking the sensual areas of
each other's bodies,
and you are anxious to fulfill your sexual craving.

Suddenly you are together,
as one,
and you reach a beautiful sexual climax that
engulfs both of you,
and satisfies you in every way.

You lie on the bed together and think of the
wonders of the world and the overpowering beauty
you have just experienced.

The warm glow of the light entering the room
begins to fade,

and you drift off into a peaceful sleep in each other's arms.

You begin to dream about your wonderful sexual experience,
and you relive the passion once again in your dreams.

When you awaken in the morning,
light filters through the window.

You can hear birds singing in the fields that surround the castle.

Again,
strong passions come over you, and you make love again with wild abandon.

After you have reached a peak of excitement, you both lie back and rest for what seems to be an endless time.

You think about all the sexual excitement you have experienced,
and know that you have been sexually fulfilled.

This transcript could be altered or extended according to your own tastes and desire. What is exciting for one person may not be for another. Whatever your preferences are, incorporate them in your transcript, in as varied and imaginative a way as possible. Explicit sexual details of your bodies as well as descriptions of your sexual acts may be appropriate for you.

It is important to remember that Total Mind Power techniques are *not* based on will power or concentration. In fact, trying too hard to reach sexual goals may be counter-productive in the case of a man suffering from impotence or a woman unable to achieve orgasm.

Relax, and let Total Mind Power lead you to the fulfillment of your sexual desires to a greater extent than ever before.

REFERENCES

Annon, J.S., "The Behavioral Treatment of Sexual Problems, Vol. 1, Brief Therapy." Honolulu: Kapiolani Health Services, 1974.

Comfort, A., Primary Care for Six Basic Sexual Problems, "Modern Medicine," December, 1974, 25.

Cooper, A.J., Factors in Male Sexual Inadequacy: A Review. "Journal of Nervous and Mental Disease," 1969, 149:337-359.

Faulk, M., 'Frigidity.' A Critical Review. "Archives of Sexual Behavior," 1973, 2:257-266.

Ferinden, W.E. and Tugender, H.S., "A Handbook of Hypno-Operant Therapy and Other Behavior Therapy Techniques Manual No. 2: The Management of Sexual Disorders." South Orange, N.J.: Power Publishers, Inc., 1972.

Fisher, S., "Understanding the Female Orgasm." New York: Basic Books, 1973.

Greenson, R., Fisher, C., Bonime, W., Ullman, M., Kramer, M. and Noble, D., What Is the Significance of Sexual Dreams? "Medical Aspects of Human Sexuality," 1975, 9:12-27.

Henson, D.E. and Rubin, H.B., Voluntary Control of Eroticism. "Journal of Applied Behavior Analysis," 1971, 4:37-44.

Kaplan, H.S., "The New Sex Therapy." New York: Brunner and Mazel, 1974.

Katchadourian, H.A. and Lunde, D.T., "Fundamentals of Human Sexuality." New York: Holt, Rinehart, and Winston, 1972.

Kinsey, A.C., Pomery, W.B. and Martin, C.E., "Sexual Behavior in the Human Male." Philadelphia: W.B. Saunders Company, 1948.

Kinsey, A.C., Pomeroy, W.B., Martin, C.E. and Gebhard, P.H., "Sexual Behavior in the Human Female." Philadelphia: W.B. Saunders Company, 1953.

Kraft, T. and Al-Issa, I., Behavior Therapy and the Treatment of Frigidity. "American Journal of Psychotherapy," 1967, 21:116-120.

Kroger, W.S., Psychosomatic Aspects of Frigidity and Impotency. "International Record of Medicine," 1958, 171:469-478.

Laws, D.R. and Rubin, H.B., Instructional Control of an Autonomic Sexual Response. "Journal of Applied Behavior Analysis," 1969, 2:93-99.

Lazarus, A., Treatment of Chronic Frigidity by Systematic Desensitization. "Journal of Nervous and Mental Disease," 1963.

MacVaugh, G., "Frigidity: Successful Treatment in One Hypnotic Imprint Session with the Oriental Relaxation Technique." New York: Medcon Inc., 1972.

Masters, W.H. and Johnson, V.E., "Human Sexual Inadequacy." Boston: Little, Brown, 1970.

Osborne, D., Behavioral Treatment of Orgasmic Inadequacy. "Medical Clinics of North America," 1974, 58:857-860.

Perlmutter, J.F., Rosenbaum, M., Shearer, M.R., Glaser, H.H. and Heiman, J., Do Women Always Know When They Had an Orgasm? "Medical Aspects of Human Sexuality," 1975, 9-12:32-44.

Razani, J., Ejaculatory Incompetence Treated by Deconditioning Anxiety. "Journal of Behavior Therapy and Experimental Psychiatry," 1972, 3:65.

Rosen, R.C., Shapiro, D., Schwartz, G.E., Voluntary Control of Penile Tumescence. "Psychosomatic Medicine," 1975, 37:479-483.

Sullivan, P.R., What Is the Role of Fantasy in Sex? "Medical Aspects of Human Sexuality," 1969, 3:79.

Uddenberg, N.J., Psychological Aspects of Sexual Inadequacy in Women. "Journal of Psychosomatic Research," 1974, 18:33-47.

CHAPTER 25:
USING TOTAL MIND POWER FOR EMOTIONAL
STABILITY AND THE DEVELOPMENT OF YOUR
FULL POTENTIAL.

You will probably first use Total Mind Power for
a specific problem in your life. However, you will
notice that there is a bonus of several general benefits in areas to which you have not directed your
mind. As you notice increased stability in your life,
as you find yourself with a more relaxed attitude
toward others, you will realize some of the positive
benefits of Total Mind Power.

Because emotional instability is a serious problem
in the tense world of today, directions for achieving
stability will prove helpful for most of us.

A young woman complained to me one day that
she was having serious problems in her life because of
a lack of self-confidence.

June had attended mind control groups and meditation groups, but still was extremely embarrassed if
she had to stand and talk in front of a group, or even
walk into a roomful of people.

The problem had grown so large in her mind

that June had begun to believe she was mentally ill, and was seeking help from a psychologist.

When I presented to her the possibility of using her own mind to overcome her timidity she was skeptical, but willing to try, because her whole life was being made miserable by her lack of self-confidence and her great sense of insecurity.

After a month of using Total Mind Power techniques, June's attitude and personality had changed markedly for the better, and she reported her emotional stability was greater than it had ever been.

She found she had to use the techniques about three times a week to maintain her confidence, but said they were so easy and convenient that she saw no problem with their continued use, especially since she felt she was being helped in other areas, was developing a more positive attitude toward life and was becoming more creative.

Although the use of Total Mind Power techniques for any purpose tends to offer by-products of general well-being and greater serenity, specific directions for a particular result always are the most effective.

The following transcript is a model for those seeking greater emotional stability, and to develop their fullest potential:

You are becoming more self-confident and positive about matters in your life than you were in the past.

You are developing an emotional stability that gives you the ability to carry out your daily tasks, and more strength in coping with everyday situations.

You are much less anxious and far more relaxed about your life.

You are therefore less worried or depressed.

You notice that because of your ability to relax
your mind and clear your thoughts,
your alertness and intelligence increase,
and you are able to remember things more clearly
than ever before.

Your capacity to clear your mind also gives
you more creativity.

You have new ideas about the directions of
your life.

The way you look at yourself is improving,
and therefore you have greater tolerance toward
other people in your life.

As your thinking becomes more and more positive,
you go about your life in a natural and relaxed way.

Your learning ability is improving,
and you are able to better comprehend the things that
you read and hear.

If you are a student,
you find that you are able to concentrate on your
studies to a greater degree.

Because of your increased learning ability,
memory capacity and expanded ability to perceive,

your grades improve and you feel more comfortable
about school in general.

You also find that you are developing the
ability to solve your school problems,
as well as your everyday problems,
more quickly and accurately.

You develop more energy and zest for living,
and this gives you more strength with which to
complete the work of your life.

Your dependency on others decreases,
and you become more self-sufficient and independent.

You are able to act rapidly and make decisions
more quickly on matters that occur in your life.

You are able to perceive the motivations of
others around you,
and you therefore become more aware of your total
circumstances and relationships to other people.

Because of your new understanding and
perception about other people,
you develop a growing tolerance toward their
inadequacies.

You realize their needs, and you have a feeling
for their problems as well as your own.

You begin to see most people as basically good,

and you develop a capacity for warmer interpersonal relationships.

You begin to see the humorous side of human nature,
and you no longer take unimportant things too seriously.

You begin to develop a better understanding of yourself and of those around you.

Since you are becoming more relaxed around other people,
you find yourself developing a friendliness toward other people.

You find yourself smiling more than you have.

You are feeling more positive about yourself, and developing an inner control that gives you a quiet assurance about your actions.

You develop spontaneous warmth and a giving attitude toward those around you.

And your understanding and feeling for your environment—and your fellow man—is enhanced.

The quality of your entire life is improved and you develop a growing satisfaction with your potential.

There is harmony in your life . . . much more than before.

This makes you more productive.

You are getting a broadened outlook on life, which brings you enriching experiences.

This enriched thinking and understanding creates contentment, and eliminates feelings of irritability and anxiety.

Since there is less stress in your life than before you started using Total Mind Power, you feel more fulfilled in your work.

Your efficiency and effectiveness increase.

You are generating unbounded energy, and you project liveliness and radiance.

The workings of your mind give you excellent reactions to life, and to the processes of your thinking.

Through your Total Mind Power all of these benefits are increased in your life to an unlimited extent.

Your achievements become more impressive with every passing day as you continue to grow toward your full potential.

REFERENCES

Beary, J.F. and Benson, H., A Simple Psychophysiologic Technique Which Elicits the Hypometabolic Changes of the Relaxation Response. "Psychosomatic Medicine," 1974, 36:115-120.

Dawley, H.H., Anxiety Reduction Through Self-Administered Relaxation. "Psychological Reports," 1975, 36:595-597.

Deibert, A.N. and Harmon, A.I., "New Tools for Changing Behavior." Chicago: Research Press, 1970.

Forrest, M. and Kroth, J.A., Psychometric and Physiological Indices for Anxiety. "Journal of Clinical Psychology," 1971, 27:40-42.

Green, E. and Green, A., Mind Training, ESP, Hypnosis and Voluntary Control of Internal States. "The Academy of Parapsychology and Medicine," 1973.

Jacobson, E., "Modern Treatment of Tense Patients." Springfield, Illinois: Charles C. Thomas, Publisher, 1970.

Jacobson, E. (ed.), "Tension in Medicine." Springfield, Illinois: Charles C. Thomas, Publisher, 1967.

Kanfer, F.H., The Maintenance of Behavior by Self-Generated Stimuli and Reinforcement. A. Jacobs and L. Sachs (eds.), "The Psychology of Private Elements." New York: Academic Press, 1971.

Klausner, S.Z. (ed.), "The Quest for Self-Control." New York: Free Press, 1965.

Maltz, M., "The Magic Power of Self-Image Psychology." Englewood Cliffs, N.J.: Prentice-Hall, Inc., 1964.

Melville, C.H., Systematic Desensitization: The roles of Muscular Relaxation and Positive Mental Imagery. "Dissertation Abstracts International," 1972, 32:4864.

Nicassio, P. and Bootzin, R., A Comparison of Progressive Relaxation and Autogenic Training as Treatments for Insomnia. "Journal of Abnormal Psychology," 1974, 83:253-260.

Selye, H., "The Stress of Life." New York: McGraw-Hill Book Company, 1956.

Shallice, T., Dual Functions of Consciousness, "Psychological Review," 1972, 79:383-393.

CHAPTER 26:
HOW TO USE TOTAL MIND POWER TO INCREASE
YOUR EXTRASENSORY PERCEPTION.

The term "extra-sensory perception" does not necessarily indicate supranormal or supernatural powers. The words describe an extension of your senses, a quality most people probably already have but do not use, just as they do not fully use their mental potential.

Whether or not actual ESP exists as a supranormal function has not been proved scientifically so far, but Total Mind Power can help you increase your perceptiveness in relation to the world around you.

With the aid of Total Mind Power you can learn to "read" the people you meet, more quickly and accurately, because of a heightening of your senses, and a honing of the intuition that acts for all of us at some time. Whether or not you can develop the ability to read someone's mind or look into the future is for you to decide.

Increasing your perceptiveness will heighten your ability to make decisions, improve your relationships with your friends and family. Where you go beyond that point is up to you.

I met a young college graduate who was in a middle-management spot in a corporation that required a long term of working one's way up the corporate ladder.

The conversation turned to ESP and parapsychology, and I was amazed to discover that Robert had no interest in these subjects and considered them lacking in any practical function. As the conversation continued he seemed to be actually frightened by the topic, and sought to avoid further discussion.

I could not understand his attitude because I believed increased sensitivity would be invaluable in his job. There have been several articles published about the nature of decision-making that have referred to the "sixth sense" successful businessmen and corporate executives seem to possess, which permits them to assess a situation correctly and make a quick and effective decision about it.

When I developed the conversation along those lines, Robert suddenly became interested and began asking about ways to develop extra-sensory perception. We discussed the fact that successful people often seem to have hunches and the courage to act on them, and he asked me more about Total Mind Power, to which I had referred in our conversation.

Several months later Robert called to tell me that he had tried Total Mind Power techniques and was tremendously pleased over the increase in his decision-making ability, an increase that had led to a promotion.

Development of extra-sensory perception is useful in other ways also, especially in helping to make correct judgments of the persons you encounter in daily life.

Young women, and men too, have often told me how they have been "fooled" by persons they have met. They had been totally deceived time after time about the real character and intent of the other persons until they had been hurt.

Once you have developed your innate "sixth sense" you will be able to sense desirable or undesirable situations in your surroundings more quickly. You will have a better understanding of the nature of the people around you, so you can relate to them and enter into more pleasant personal relationships. Development of your full potential for human understanding will help you get along much better in the world.

The following transcript is a guide for using Total Mind Power to increase your ability to use your undeveloped "sixth sense" to pick up those extra clues about your own life, and the life around you, that lead to richer living:

You think about a person you know whom you would like to learn more about.

You visualize every detail about this person in your mind.

You remember everything about the individual, and project this image onto a screen in the front of your mind.

You see every one of the person's movements, gestures and actions.

You now have a complete picture of the person in a physical sense, and you notice all of the physical qualities from head to toes.

You see the clothing,
the color of the hair and the way it's combed
and styled.

You see all the details of this person's facial
expressions,
even the manner in which the head is held.

You focus your attention on the eyes,
and you look deeply into them.

You notice all of the eye movements as well
as the eyelid and eyebrow gestures.

You take in every aspect of the person's face.

You notice all of the different ways the person
holds shoulders and hands,
and you can see the hands in great detail as you
study the lines and the positions of the palms and
fingers.

Even the person's walk gives you an idea about
his nature.

After visualizing all of these things in your mind,
you form some general thoughts about the person,
such as where he came from,
what his attitudes and motives are,
and what direction the person's life is taking.

You perceive the various attitudes of the person

and you balance them while forming an evaluation
of the person's make-up.

You direct your mind to see the color you would
attribute to the person's personality.

You imagine this color in an aura around the
person,
and you look at it to see what shades and tones are
present.

You know that a calm and relaxed individual
would probably be surrounded by a blue,
green or deep blue-green aura.

A person who is nervous and anxious tends to
show a red,
yellowish or orange color.

You also know that if a person is ill,
he may have colors around him that seem washed out
or uneven.

You think about the health of the person and
what types of problems he may have had in the past.

You focus your mind very,
very closely on the person in every detail,
and you imagine all of the characteristics of his life.

You let your mind freely imagine these things
as you get a picture in your mind about the
individual's lifestyle.

You now visualize him in an imaginary situation created by your mind,
perhaps a situation where you are meeting the person for the first time.

You notice his actions,
characteristics and attitudes when you meet.

You form an impression about the person's mental attitude toward you.

After you have completed this image,
you hold it in your mind until you have a chance to meet and talk with him again.

After several Total Mind Power experiences of this kind, you will see an increase in your perceptions. You'll begin to observe people in a way you never have before, and to notice events to which you were previously oblivious. Applying this new perception in group situations can be extremely exciting, not to mention its entertainment value.

If you wish to experiment with other forms of extra-sensory perception, try to pick up words or symbols that are being sent to you by another person. Ask a friend to think of a simple geometric symbol or symbols. Use Total Mind Power to focus your mind on visualizing these symbols. The results may amaze you.

If you consistently pick up more than five of 25 symbols someone else is trying to transmit to you, you are scoring above average, which may indicate you are perceiving with extra-sensory ability.

There is no doubt that your perception in all areas will increase tremendously the more you use Total Mind Power to increase your extra-sensory potential.

REFERENCES

Beloff, J., "Research in Parapsychology." Metuchen, N.J.: The Scarecrow Press, 1973.

Christopher, M., "ESP, Seers and Psychics." New York: Thomas Y. Crowell Co., 1970.

Christopher, M., "Mediums, Mystics and the Occult." New York: Thomas Y. Crowell Co., 1975.

Friedman, J., Gantz, L. and Sinclair, P., Training Groups to Develop ESP Abilities. "Parapsychology Review," 1973, 4:10-14.

Green, E. and Green, A., Mind Training, ESP, Hypnosis, and Voluntary Control of Internal States. "Special Report—The Academy of Parapsychology and Medicine," Los Altos, California, 1973.

Hansel, C.E.M., "ESP: A Scientific Evaluation." New York: Scribners, 1966.

Kreitler, H. and Kreitler, S., Subliminal Preception and Extrasensory Perception. "Journal of Parapsychology," 1973, 37:163-188.

LeShan, L., "The Medium, The Mystic, and The Physicist." New York: Ballantine Books, 1974.

Monroe, R., "Journeys Out of the Body." New York: Doubleday, 1971.

Osis, K. and Bokert, E., ESP and Changed States of Consciousness Induced by Meditation. "Journal of the American Society of Psychical Research," 1971, 65:17-65.

Ostrander, S. and Schroeder, L., "Psychic Discoveries Behind the Iron Curtain." New York: Bantam Books, 1971.

Palmer, J., Scoring in ESP Tests as a Function of Belief in ESP. "Journal of the American Society for Psychical Research," 1971, 65:373-408.

Pratt, J.G., "ESP Research Today." Metuchen, N.J.: The Scarecrow Press, 1973.

Rhine, L.E., "PSI." New York: Harper and Row, Publishers, 1975.

Ryzl, M., "Parapsychology Today: A Geographic View." New York: Parapsychology Foundation, 1973.

Schmeidler, G., "Extrasensory Perception." New York: Atherton Press, 1974.

CHAPTER 27:
GENERAL BENEFITS FROM THE USE OF TOTAL MIND POWER.

In the preceding chapters you have learned to use Total Mind Power techniques to control specific problems as well as to bring a feeling of harmony and purpose into your life. In this application you have set aside a particular time and followed a particular pattern, which is practical and advantageous when working on long-term solutions.

However, problems often arise unexpectedly. Everyone's life presents a series of crises and traumas during which it is handy to have a quick tool for calming the nerves and resolving a difficulty. Total Mind Power, your own private remedy for your private ills, is a versatile and adaptable answer for these situations.

In a traumatic situation such as an accident, you can use Total Mind Power to relieve your anxiety and tension, and also any resulting pain.

Total Mind Power can be used any time, anywhere, for any length of time. A brief moment of focusing awareness in the midst of a busy or confusing day will give you new strength to go about your daily tasks.

Because an important part of the Total Mind Power techniques is Step Three, repetition, you inevitably will have stored away in your memory much, if not all, of the transcripts you have used.

When a need arises you will be able to remember and repeat to yourself a condensation of the words and phrases of the appropriate transcript. Your mind will automatically have condensed it for retention so that a 30-minute recording will run through your mind in a few minutes.

In competitive situations, such as important business conferences or a game of golf or tennis, this application of Total Mind Power is especially valuable. To relax your mind and help you concentrate on the task at hand, use Total Mind Power techniques for as little as three minutes, either before you go into competition or during it.

Once you have developed techniques for specific problems, they are always at hand to help you with similar problems, or to be adapted to new ones.

Some benefits are nebulous—slowing down the aging process and achieving better health, for instance —and the exact effects of Total Mind Power in these areas cannot be measured, but there are strong indications that the benefits described herein are tremendous.

More tangible benefits include increased awareness; greater sensitivity to, and ability to deal with, the people around you; expansion of your personality; increased adaptability, an ability to accept situations calmly and to retain your sense of proportion in crises and an increased confidence in yourself that causes you to radiate a more positive attitude.

REFERENCES

Barber, T.X., Implications for Human Capabilities and Potentialities: Training in Human Potentialities. "Biofeedback and Self-Control 1974," 1975, 5:63-71.

Barron, F., "Creativity and Psychological Health." Princeton: Van Nostrand, 1963.

Bronowski, J., "The Ascent of Man." Boston: Little-Brown, 1974.

Brown, B.B., Recognition of Aspects of Consciousness Through Association With EEG Alpha Activity Represented by a Light Signal. "Psychophysiology," 1970, 6:442-452.

Clarke, P.R.F. and Spear, F.G., Reliability and Sensitivity in the Self-Assessment of Well Being. "Bulletin of the British Psychological Society," 1964, 17:55.

Eisenman, R., Critique of Treatment of Insomnia by Relaxation Training. Relaxation Training, Rogerian Therapy or Demand Characteristics. "Journal of Ab Normal Psychology," 1970, 75:315-316.

Foulkes, D., Mental Activity in Relaxed Wakefulness. "Journal of Abnormal Psychology," 1975, 84:66-75.

French, A.P., Therapeutic Application of a Simple Relaxation Method. "American Journal of Psychotherapy," 1974, 28:282-287.

Gaarder, K., Control of States of Consciousness. I. Attainment Through Control of Psychophysiological Variables. II. Attainment Through External Feedback Augmenting Control of Psychophysiological Variables. "Archives of General Psychiatry, 1971, 25:429-441.

Green, E., Biofeedback for Mind-Body Self-Regulation: Healing and Creativity. "Biofeedback and Self-Control," 1973, 152-166.

Hord, D., Naitoh, P. and Johnson, L.C., Intensity and Coherence Contours During Self-Regulated High Alpha Activity. "Electroencephalography and Clinical Neurophysiology," 1972, 32:429-433.

Hord, D., Naitoh, P. and Johnson, L.C., EEG Spectral Features of Self-Regulated High Alpha States. "Psychophysiology," 1972, 9:278.

Houston, B.K., Control Over Stress, Locus of Control and Response to Stress. "Journal of Personality and Social Psychology," 1972, 21:249-255.

Kamiya, J., Conscious Control of Brain Waves. "Psychology Today," 1968, 1:

Kanfer, F.H., Self-Regulation: Research Issues and Speculations. C. Neuringer and J.L. Michael (eds.) "Behavior Modification and Clinical Psychology." New York: Appleton-Century-Crofts, 1970.

Krippner, S. and Hughes, W., Dreams and Human Potential "Journal of Humanistic Psychology," 1970, 10:1;20.

Lazarus, R.S., Psychological Stress and Coping in Adaptation and Illness. "International Journal of Psychiatry in Medicine," 1974, 5:321-333.

Maltz, M., "Creative Living for Today." New York: Simon and Schuster, Inc., 1967.

Marshall, W.L., The Role of Mental Relaxation in Experimental Desensitization. "Behavior Research and Therapy," 1972, 10:355-366.

McKellar, P., "Imagination and Thinking." London: Cohen & West, 1957.

Nicassio, P., A Comparison of Progressive Relaxation and Autogenic Training as Treatments for Insomnia. "Journal of Abnormal Psychology," 1974, 83:253-260.

Rogers, C., "On Becoming a Person." Boston: Houghton Mifflin Company, 1961.

Rosenfeld, J.P., Rudell, A.P. and Fox, S.S., Operant Control of Neural Events in Humans. "Science," 1969, 165:821-823.

Sacks, B., Fenwick, P.B.C., Marks, J., Fenton, G.W.and Hebden, A., An Investigation of the Phenomenon of Auto-Control of the Alpha Rhythm and Possible and Associated Feeling States Using Visual Feedback. "Electroencephalography and Clinical Neurophysiology," 1972, 32:461-463.

Schechter, N., Schmeidler, G. and Staal, M., Dream Reports and Creative Tendencies in Students of the Arts, Sciences, and Engineering. "Journal of Consulting Psychology," 1965, 29:415.

Snaith, R.P., A Method of Psychotherapy Based on Relaxation Techniques. "British Journal of Psychiatry," 1974, 124:473.

Thorne, F.C., Introspective Analysis of Self-Functioning. "Journal of Clinical Psychology," 1974, 30:231-233.

Watzlawick, P., Weakland, J. and Fisch, R., "Change: Principles of Problem Formation and Problem Resolution." New York: W.W. Norton, 1974.

CHAPTER 28:
THE USE OF TOTAL MIND POWER FOR GROUPS
AND SOCIETY.

Most of this book has been dedicated to the use of
Total Mind Power for the benefit of the individual.
Having discovered its value, you may want to share
the techniques with your friends, either on an individual or a group basis.

Sharing transcripts and techniques increases the
imaginative quality for everyone. Many persons enjoy
participating in group activities, and will derive great
benefit from a shared effort.

If you are working in a group, recorded transcripts may be played for everyone to hear, or you
may trade your recordings for similar problems. The
use of several different transcripts for the same problem, providing as it does a wider variety of approaches
than one person might imagine, may increase the beneficial effects.

If all the members of a group are interested in
cooperating on a single transcript for a problem all
share, you may develop an extremely imaginative and

creative recording. This transcript might be written out, with all the directions incorporated and coordinated, and then recorded by one person, or by each person adding a voice. If the transcript is to be used in a group it should be worded for group participation, and you might all be directed to hold hands and focus your awareness together.

Since Total Mind Power, even when used individually, leads to a better understanding between people, how much greater might be its efficacy in lessening tensions and fostering more comfortable group situations, if the entire group shared the techniques as a unit.

Several years ago I was talking to a group on a university campus about greater use of the mind. One of the girls in the group said that she, two other girls and three male students were living together in a large house and sharing expenses and work equally, but that discords over minor problems kept recurring. She wondered if Total Mind Power could help smooth out the discords.

I suggested the six might find it enjoyable to construct transcripts aimed at helping them to live together more harmoniously, and gave her some suggestions on how to proceed.

The next time I saw her she told me that the making of new transcripts, and listening to old ones relating to their difficulties, had become a weekly ritual. She said things were much more harmonious, and that the members of the group were helping each other construct transcripts for specific personal problems.

One of the boys was suffering from migraine headaches. The other five had helped him construct a Total Mind Power transcript that directed his mind to overcome the problem, and his headaches were becoming less and less frequent.

All members of the group were gaining a new confidence in the power of their own minds to help them with their problems of daily living.

Whenever groups of people can overcome their mutual anxieties and tensions, their ability to communicate and to get along with each other increases. All of the individual benefits of Total Mind Power work equally for groups who adopt its principles.

The most important tool an individual has for improving his physical health and mental well-being is his own mind, the potential of which has barely been touched. If one person, working alone, awakening the sleeping portions of his mind, can dramatically change his life, how much greater will be the effect of thousands of minds, working both individually and collectively, for health, harmony and successful living for all.

REFERENCES

Aponte, J.F. and Aponte, C.E., Group Preprogrammed Systematic Desensitization Without the Simultaneous Presentation of Aversive Scenes With Relaxation Training. "Behavior Research and Therapy," 1971, 9:337-346.

Archer, J., Fiester, T., Kagan, N., Rate, L., Spierling, T. and VanNoord, R., New Method for Education Treatment and Research in Human Interaction. "Journal of Consulting Psychology," 1972, 19:275-281.

Brandes, N.S. and Gardner, M.L. (eds.), "Group Therapy for the Adolescent." New York: Jason Aronson, Inc., 1973.

Combs, A.W., Avila, D.L. and Purkey, W.W., "Helping Relationships." Boston: Allyn & Bacon, 1972.

Clynes, M., Toward a View of Man. M. Clynes and J. Milsum (eds.), "Bio-Medical Engineering Systems." New York: McGraw-Hill Book Company, 1970.

Giora, Z., Psychosomatics: Promise and Fulfillment. "British Journal of Medical Psychology," 1972, 45: 203-207.

Green, E. and Green, A., The Ins and Outs of Mind-Body Energy. "Science Year 1974, World Book Science Annual." Chicago: Field Enterprises Educational Co., 1973, p.146.

Hall, H.V., Effects of Direct and Self-Reinforcement as a Function of Internal-External Control. "Perceptual and Motor Skills," 1973, 37:753-754.

Heaton, R.C., The Relationship Between Self-Esteem, Self-Reinforcement and the Internal-External Personality Dimension. "Journal of Genetic Psychology," 1973, 123:3.

Hjelle, L.A., Transcendental Meditation and Psychological Health. "Perceptual and Motor Skills," 1974, 39:623-628.

Lipowski, Z.J., Psychosomatic Medicine in a Changing Society: Some Current Trends in Theory and Research. "Comprehensive Psychiatry," 1973, 14:203-215.

Maslow, A.H., A Theory of Meta-Motivation: The Biological Rooting of Value-Life. A.J. Sutich and M.A. Villch (eds.), "Readings in Humanistic Psychology." New York: Free Press, 1969.

McLuhan, M., "Understanding Media: The Extensions of Man." New York: McGraw-Hill Book Company, 1964.

Meissner, W.W., The Role of Imitative Social Learning in Identification Processes. "Journal of the American Psychoanalytic Association," 1974, 22:512-536.

Muses, C. and Young, A.M. (eds.), "Consciousness and Reality: The Human Pivot Point." New York: Outerbridge and Lazard, 1972.

Rozensky, R.H., Behavior Change and Individual Differences in Self-Control. "Behavior Research and Therapy," 1974, 12:267-268.

Spear, J.E., The Utilization of Non-Drug Induced Altered States of Consciousness in Borderline Recidivists. "The American Journal of Clinical Hypnosis," 1975, 18:111-126.

Switzky, H.N., Motivational Orientation and the Relative Efficacy of Self-Monitored and Externally Imposed Reinforcement Systems in Children. "Journal of Personality and Social Psychology," 30:360-366.

Toffler, A., "Future Shock." New York: Randon House, 1970.

Towsend, R.E., A Comparison of Biofeedback-Mediated Relaxation and Group Therapy in the Treatment of Chronic Anxiety. "American Journal of Psychiatry," 1975, 132:598-601.

CHAPTER 29:
USING TOTAL MIND POWER TO ENHANCE
YOUR RELIGIOUS EXPERIENCES.

A friend took me to lunch a few years ago and we discussed a problem he was having with finding meaning in his life.

He said that he had always been a very religious person, but now found that he had drifted away from his church and his beliefs. He no longer felt close to God.

I asked him if he felt that God played any part in his life, and he said that he had so lost contact with God that he could no longer feel God influencing his life.

I asked my friend if he had ever considered using more of his mind to increase his awareness of God, and reminded him of the belief that most people use only 10 percent of their mental potential.

He agreed that most people probably do use only a very small percentage of their minds, but said he was not aware there was any established way to increase that percentage, and that he certainly did not see any way to use his mind to come close to God.

I described Total Mind Power techniques to him, and he said he would try them, since he desperately wanted once more to feel God's presence influencing his life.

Several months later my friend called to thank me. He said he had found a new interest in his church, and had recently been elected to a church board.

He said he had used Total Mind Power techniques as part of his prayer sessions and had developed a new and more powerful feeling for God than he had before. His only regret was that he had not known the techniques earlier in his life. He was so delighted with the results he had achieved that he was introducing Total Mind Power techniques to his Sunday School classes, with great success.

Whatever your religious faith, whatever your relationship to God, it can be enriched through the application of your mind. You can increase your inspiration, strengthen your belief, make your worship more meaningful, heighten your prayer experience, intensify God's involvement in your life, in all ways reinforce the teachings of your particular faith.

The religious leaders and writers within your faith can supply many ideas. The details of procedure will vary from faith to faith and individual to individual, but the following Step Two transcript is a useful model for increasing your inspiration and feeling of closeness to God. More than one area of need may be combined in the same transcript, and the use of Total Mind Power techniques in groups may help unify those of the same faith:

In your mind's eye you create a picture of a beautiful beach,

and you see yourself walking along the sand.
It's warm and peaceful,
and you decide to take off your shoes and
stockings and feel the sand between your toes and
the cooling touch of the little waves as they gently flow across the sand and break around your
ankles.

Several small birds are running along beside you.
You can hear them making little whistling noises.
The air is filled with the odors of the seashore,
and you can taste the salt spray on your lips.

As you look out over the ocean you marvel at
the immenseness of the world;
you feel a great sense of wonder about the universe
and an overpowering sensation of oneness with the
Creator.

As you continue to walk along the beach you
are overjoyed by the wonders of God's creation
around you.

You reach a path that leads up a green hill,
and decide to climb the path.

When you reach the top of the hill you find
yourself looking out over a vast panorama of sand
and water.

In the distance you see dolphins leaping out
of the water as they play,
and you marvel at the complexity of God's creatures.
You begin to realize that you are one of those
marvels,
a unique creation.
An appreciation for God's works fills you with
a surging sense of enlightenment and rejoicing.
Your faith is renewed and you become deeply
aware of God as a presence in your everyday life.

There is a gentle,
grassy slope on the far side of the hill.
You lie down in the grass and look up to where
seagulls arc swooping gracefully,
silhouetted against the light blue sky.

The sun dips toward the horizon,
turning the sky to a pure gold that reminds you of
the perfection of God's works.
As the sun sinks lower and dusk approaches,
you see the stars coming out and you feel a sense
of awe.

You revel in the sense of the majesty of God's universe,
and experience a greater awareness of God's power in your own life.

Your joy seems to increase as each new star appears.

You become deeply conscious of God's strength and purpose and you know you are going to direct your life more purpusefully from now on.

You feel a unity with God that gives you an abiding trust in his mercy and goodness.

Your entire being tunes in to the reality of God's presence as an ever-present force in your life.

You are filled with enthusiasm for the new direction and inspiration this closeness to God has given you.

You know now that whenever you need new inspiration,
you will be able to think back on this time and experience the closeness to God you are feeling now,
to renew your faith and strengthen your purpose in life.

REFERENCES

Ames, E.S., "The Psychology of Religious Experience. New York: Houghton Mifflin Co., 1910.

Arnett, W.E., "Religion and Judgement: An Essay on the Method and Meaning of Religion." New York: Appleton-Century-Crofts, 1966.

Barton, K., Personality Variables as Predictors of Attitudes Toward Science and Religion. "Psychological Reports," 1973, 32:223-228.

Belgum, D.R., "Religion and Medicine: Essays on Meaning, Values and Health." Ames, Iowa: Iowa Stare Univ. Press, 1967.

Bem, D.J., "Beliefs, Attitudes and Human Affairs."Belmont, California: Brooks-Cole Publishing Co., 1970.

Brena, S.F., "Pain and Religion: A Psychophysiological Study." Springfield, Ill.: Charles C. Thomas, Publisher, 1972.

Coates, T.J., Personality Correlates of Religious Commitment: A Further Verification' "Journal of Social Psychology," 1973, 89:159-160.

Dawson, J.H., The Master's Touch. "Journal of the Tennessee Medical Association," 1975, 68:699-704.

Dominic Brother, Visual Imagery and Religious Ceremonial. "Perceptual and Motor Skills," 1975, 40:18-25.

Farkas, H., Therapeutic Spiritual Experiences. "American Journal of Psychiatry," 1973, 130:1045-1046.

Gassert, R.G., "Psychiatry and Religious Faith." New York: Viking Press, 1964.

Hedley, G.P., "Religion and the Natural World." Seattle: The University of Washington Press, 1962.

Hein, G.W., Psychotherapy and the Spiritual Dimension of Man. "Psychotherapy and Psychosomatics," 1974, 24: 482-489.

Hjelle, L.A., Relationship of a Measure of Self-Actualization to Religious Participation. "Journal of Psychology," 1975, 89:179-182.

Horosz, W., "Escape From Destiny: Self-Directive Theory of Man and Culture." Springfield, Ill.: Charles C. Thomas, Publisher, 1967.

James, W., "The Varieties of Religious Experience: A Study in Human Nature." New York: New American Library, 1958.

Lenski, G.E., "The Religious Factor: A Sociological Study of Religion's Impact on Politics, Economics and Family Life." Garden City, N.Y.: Doubleday dna Company, Inc., 1963.

Minirth, F., The Effects of Religious Backgrounds on Emotional Problems. "Journal of the Arkansas Medical Association," 1975, 72:227-234.

Needleman, J., "The New Religions." Garden City, N.Y.: Doubleday dn Company, Inc., 1970.

Pattison, E.M., Faith Healing: A Study of Personality and Function. "Journal of Nervous and Mental Disease," 1973, 157:397-409.

Radhakrishnan, S., "Recovery of Faith." New York: Harper and Row, Publishers, 1955.

Rizzuto, A.M., Object Relations and the Formation of the Image of God. "British Journal of Medical Psychology." 1974, 47:83-99.

Schar, H., "Religion and the Cure of Souls in Jung's Psychology." New York: Pantheon Books, 1950.

Schneider, L., "Religion, Culture and Society: A Reader in the Sociology of Religion." New York: John Wiley and Sons, Inc., 1964.

Simenstad, J.O., The Role of Faith in Medical Practice: A Physician's Viewpoint. "Wisconsin Medical Journal," 1974, 73:7-10.

Smith, H., "The Religions of Man." New York: Harper and Row, Publishers, 1958.

Smith, H.W., "Man and His Gods." Boston: Little, Brown and Company, 1952.

Tillich, P., "Dynamics of Faith." New York: Harper and Row, Publishers, 1957.

Van Buskirk, J.D., "Religion, Healing and Health." New York: The Macmillan Company, 1952.

Van Kaam, A.L., "The Rhythm of Involvement and Detachment in Daily Life." Denville, N.J.: Dimension Books, 1970.

Weatherhead, L.D., "Psychology, Religion and Healing." London: Hodder and Stoughton, 1963.

Whitlen, O.R., "Religious Behavior." Englewood Cliffs, N.J.: Prentice-Hall, Inc., 1964.

Wilson, W.P., Mental Health Benefits of Religious Salvation. "Diseases of the Nervous System," 1972, 33:382-386.

Young, R.K., "Spiritual Therapy: How the Physician, Psychiatrist and Minister Collaborate in Healing." New York: Harper and Row, Publishers, 1960.

CHAPTER 30;
MOTIVATING YOURSELF TO SUCCESS WITH
TOTAL MIND POWER.

Failure seemed to be the dominant thought in my
friend's mind.

"It seems that I always fail; I never seem to do
anything right," said Walter. "I just can't seem to get
started at anything worthwhile."

Remarks like these reflected my friend's feelings
before he decided to have a try with Total Mind Power,
at my suggestion. After using Total Mind Power and
moving on to a successful career as a businessman as
well as becoming a competent sportsman, I asked
Walter for a copy of the transcript he had used that
put him on the road to positive achievement.

When he gave me the transcript he noted the
differences between Total Mind Power and other
methods he had tried. Courses, books on self-moti-
vation and positive thinking had provided him only
with partial answers and they required a lot of will
power and concentration, were not pleasant to use,
and the results were not permanent.

. Not until he used Total Mind Power, Walter said, did he find the technique for using all the potentials of his successes.

While the life around him remained the same, now he did not have to yield to its idiocyncracies, but rather was able to control situations and even manipulate or change them to his advantage. He had become master of his ship and as such was able to control his destiny rather than having it laid out by someone else. All that Walter needed was the assurance that Total Mind Power would work . . . and it did! He used the step-by-step procedures outlined in the preceding chapters and found a permanent answer to his problems.

The following Step Two transcript incorporates many of the directions my friend used in his transcript. Whatever the field in which you seek success, many of these directions will apply, and the transcript can be altered to fit any particular situation:

You picture in your mind a large theater.

You are about to walk onto the stage to receive an award for being most successful in a particular endeavor.

As you wait in the wings you think back upon some of the attitudes you have developed and the action you have taken to arrive at this momemt of success.

A great sense of accomplishment comes over you as you think how you have replaced your

negative thoughts with positive,
optimistic ones.

You attribute much of your success to your
profound change in attitude,
and you think about what has helped to motivate you.

You remember that you began by visualizing
yourself succeeding rather than failing,
and that stimulated you to seek for,
and find,
the winning pathway.

You remember,
also,
that when you released your fear of failure you
developed a tremendous feeling of self-confidence
and began to direct yourself in a more dynamic
manner.

The cumulative effect of affirmative thoughts
and actions has paid off and you have reached a
high point in your life as you prepare to walk
onto the stage.

You hear your name being called and the
audience applauding as you step forward to
receive a plaque bearing your name and a tribute
to your accomplishments.

The master of ceremonies emphasizes how you
have merited the award and you sense his admiration,
you look at the audience and feel their warmth,
encouragement and respect as they look back at you.

You experience a feeling similar to that of
having been victorious in a hard-fought competition.

You smile as you thank the host for the reward,
and you vow to yourself that you will continue
to develop new and more positive attitudes toward
whatever tasks arise in your life.

You also remember how,
at certain points in your progress toward your goal,
things seemed difficult,
but as you persisted,
you realized that accomplishment of the worthwhile
requires a continuous,
positive direction of your mind.

You decide to use Total Mind Power techniques
consistently whenever you need to apply yourself
to the achievement of a specific goal.

Now the host is handing you the plaque;
you feel its heavy wooden frame and see the engraved
words of congratulations and you have a great sense
of satisfaction.

You hear the audience applauding and are over-
whelmed with a sense of joy.

Your heart beats faster with excitement,
but you remain calm and sure of yourself.

As you thank the audience and the host for
the reward,

you become more than ever convinced that your
change to a positive mental attitude helped you
attain this honor.

You remember how you started using the phrase,
"I can do it" instead of, "I can't,"
and how almost at once you began to accomplish
more than you ever had before.

Your fears and doubts have been cast aside
and you no longer are apprehensive about the
unknown.

You realize that fear is a disease you have
decided to cast out of your life,
since it is a hindrance to you in reaching your
chosen goals.

You walk confidently off the stage,
listening to the ovation from the crowd,
and reaffirming your intention to continue to
succeed in whatever endeavor you undertake.

The realization that each success leads to
another success motivates you to cast out of your
life all negative and self-defeating thoughts and actions.

The feeling of success makes you feel better
than you have ever felt.

It is important that this Step Two transcript, like all the others, must follow a Step One transcript for focusing your awareness. And the repeated use of the transcripts as outlined in Step Three is also vitally important to your receiving the benefits of Total Mind Power.

Merely suggesting positive thoughts is ineffective. The techniques as outlined in preceding chapters should be followed closely. There is a vast difference between suggesting to yourself that you do something, and directing yourself to do it from the position of a focused awareness. The difference is the use of 10 percent versus 90 percent of your mind.

REFERENCES

Albert, D., "How to Cash in on Your Abilities." Englewood Cliffs, N.J.: Prentice-Hall, 1962.

Appleman, J.A. "How to Increase Your Money-Making Power." New York: Frederick Fell, Inc., 1964.

Bristol, C., "The Magic of Believing." Englewood Cliffs, N.J.: Prentice-Hall, Inc., 1957.

Carnegie, D., "How to Stop Worrying and Start Living." New York: Simon and Schuster, Inc., 1948.

Carnegie, D., "How to Win Friends and Influence People." New York: Simon and Schuster, Inc.,1936.

Clark, C.H., "Brainstorming: The Dynamic Way to Create Successful Ideas." New York: Doubleday, 1958.

Dunlap, K., "Habits, Their Making and Unmaking." New York: Liveright Publishing Co., 1951.

Frank, W.W. and Lapp, C.L., "How to Outsell the Born Salesman." Macmillan Publishing Company, Inc., 1959.

Germain, W.M., "The Magic Power of Your Mind." New York: Hawthorn Books, Inc., 1956.

Goldman, H., "How to Win Customers." New York: Hawthorn Books, Inc., 1957.

Haas, K.B., "How To Develop Successful Salesmen." New York: McGraw-Hill Book Company, 1957.

Hill, N., "Think and Grow Rich." New York: Hawthorn Books, Inc., 1937.

Hill, N. and Stone, W.C., "Success Through a Positive Mental Attitude." Englewood Cliffs, N.J.: Prentice-Hall, Inc., 1960.

Maltz, M., "Creative Living for Today." New York: Trident Press, Inc., 1967.

Maltz, M., "The Magic Power of Self-Image Psychology." Englewood Cliffs, N.J.: Prentice-Hall, Inc., 1964.

Mandino, O., "The Greatest Salesman In the World." New York: Frederick Fell, Inc., 1972.

McFall, R.M. and Twentyman, C.T., "Four Experiments on the Relative Contributions of Rehearsal, Modeling and Coaching to Assertion Training. "Journal of Abnormal Psychology," 1973, 81:199-218.

Murphy, J., "The Power of Your Subconscious Mind." Englewood Cliffs, N.J.: Prentice-Hall, Inc., 1963.

Peale, N.V., "The Power of Positive Thinking." Englewood Cliffs, N.J.: Prentice-Hall, Inc., 1952.

Ponder, C., "Dynamic Laws of Prosperity: Forces That Bring Riches to You." Englewood Cliffs, N.J.: Prentice Hall, 1962.

Stone, W.C., "The Success System That Never Fails." Englewood Cliffs, N.J.: Prentice-Hall, Inc., 1962.

Schuller, R.H. "Self-Love: The Dynamic Force of Success." New York: Hawthorn Books, Inc., 1969.

Willing, J., "Strategy of Earning a Better Living." New York: Rinehart and Winston, 1959.

Zimbardo, P., "The Cognitive Control of Motivation." Glenview, Ill.: Scott Foresman, 1969.

CHAPTER 31:
INCORPORATING TOTAL MIND POWER INTO
YOUR DAILY LIFE.

NOW THAT YOU HAVE DISCOVERED HOW TO USE YOUR
TOTAL MIND, DON'T LET THE BENEFITS OF TOTAL MIND
POWER BECOME A THING OF THE PAST. This valuable
resource you have uncovered—that 90 percent of your
mind—is with you all the time and should not be
shoved back into oblivion.

TOTAL MIND POWER IS NOT A ONE-SHOT, ONE-
TIME TREAT BUT ONE THAT CAN CONTINUE TO PROVIDE
YOU WITH A FEAST FOR LIFE: The continued application of Total Mind Power techniques will make you
feel more enthusiastic, give you better health, spark
your vitality, and make you a more productive person.
You will be a more vital human being if you maintain
Total Mind Power throughout your life and not let it
become a neglected part of your existence. With continued use of Total Mind Power you will experience
an upsurge of mental and physical energies and an
exhilarating sense of physical and emotional well-being.

YOU DON'T JUST READ TOTAL MIND POWER, YOU PRACTICE IT. Total Mind Power is not merely a book to read, it is a tool you put to use. When you see and feel the results after its use you will want to incorporate it into your life, to make it as vital a part of you as all your daily functions, because if you make it an everyday activity you will feel and be healthier, function better and improve on your general well-being.

THE ESSENTIAL THING TO REMEMBER IS THAT TOTAL MIND POWER IS WITH YOU THE REST OF YOUR LIFE. Once you have learned the techniques of Total Mind Power you don't have to relearn them—they become your lifelong companions. The steps as discussed in this book, focusing your awareness, directing your mind and sequencing your mind directions, always remain the same. All you have to do is apply them to your particular needs.

Using Total Mind Power can prove to be a turning point in your life; it can mean the difference from being a listless person to one filled with hope, healthy in physical and mental outlook, and better equipped to meet challenges and win them.

YOU DON'T HAVE TO LEAVE TOTAL MIND POWER AT HOME. Total Mind Power is you, your mind, so it accompanies you wherever you go. Whenever you feel the need for using it, do it! Your office, your home, a field, anywhere you are, can be the setting for settling into Total Mind Power. And if you prefer applying it with a group rather than by yourself, Total Mind Power provides that flexibility. Solo or in concert with others, Total Mind Power can be applied.

REMEMBER, THE TRANSCRIPTS IN THIS BOOK ARE MODELS AND CAN BE ALTERED. I have prepared transcripts for a variety of common situations and problems I have encountered in my consultation with patients and friends. They can be used as outlined in this book or you can alter them to help you overcome your particular problem or improve your individual situation. You are the author of your transcripts.

IF YOU ARE NOT SATISFIED WITH THE WAY THINGS ARE HAPPENING, YOU SHOULD SURVEY THE WAY YOU ARE SPENDING YOUR TIME. If you feel life is without meaning, there is little significance to what you are doing, and your busy days permit no time for doing the things you enjoy doing, then most likely it is time to readjust your lifestyle. Use Total Mind Power to help you redirect your life. . .and continue to use it until you find the satisfaction you seek.

TOTAL MIND POWER IS NEW. It is showing you how to use the 90 percent of your mind that you have long neglected. Until now only 10 percent of your mind was working for you. Now, using the techniques in this book, Total Mind Power will be working for you, for a better life.

RE-READ THIS BOOK ANYTIME YOU FEEL YOUR TECHNIQUES NEED REFRESHING. Let this book serve as your guide, your model for fulfilling your mission. It is simple, easy to comprehend. And, whenever you feel you are slipping in the proper application of Total Mind Power, set aside some time for a refresher course. Use this book and you will be on the right track again.

SOME OTHER AREAS WHERE YOU CAN APPLY TOTAL MIND POWER ARE INDICATED BELOW. I have attempted to cover a wide variety of situations, but many more exist and you can develop your own transcripts to meet them. Share them with others so they too can be benefited by them. Share your problems and how you solved them by mailing them to me in care of the publisher for inclusion in future editions of Total Mind Power. The address for sending your transcripts is listed in the back of the book.

Areas where others have applied Total Mind Power:

Improving artistic abilities
Relieving tension headaches
Remembering past events
Alleviating allergies
Retraining muscles
Controlling skin temperature
Elimination of subvocalization in reading
Increasing creativity
Relaxation training
Controlling heart arrhythmias
Influencing brain wave activity
Controlling migraine headaches
Decreasing epileptic seizures
Alpha brain wave control
Preventing muscle spasms
Changing stomach acid concentration in ulcers
Influencing the galvanic skin reflex
Learning how to play musical instruments more readily
Improving acting performance
Increasing intuitive capabilities
Command over bowel functions
Controlling acne and other skin diseases
Improving task performance
Training the visual accommodation system
Decreasing the body's response to stress

Improving and sharpening the senses
Controlling insomnia and sleep disturbances
Self-regulation of emotional problems
Becoming more aware of yourself and your surroundings
Improving mechanical skills
Heightening pleasant emotions and feelings.

APPENDICES

Additional References
Progress Chart Example

ADDITIONAL REFERENCES

Chapter 7, Focusing Awareness.

Assigioli, R., "Psychosynthesis: A Manual of Principles and Techniques." New York: Hobbs, Dorman and Co., Inc., 1965.

Lilly, J., "The Center of the Cyclone." London: Paladin, 1973.

Andersen, M. and Savary, L.M., "Passages: A Guide for Pilgrims of the Mind." New York: Harper & Row Publishers, 1973.

Barber, T.X., Spanos, N.P. and Chaves, J.F., "Hypnosis, Imagination, and Human Potentialities." New York: Pergamon Press, Inc., 1974.

Berwick, P. and Oziel, L.J., The Use of Meditation as a Behavioral Technique. "Behavior Therapy," 1973, 4:743-745.

Burns, J.M. and Ascough, J.C., A Psysiological Comparison of Two Approaches to Relaxation and Anxiety Induction. "Behavior Therapy," 1971, 2:170-176.

Conner, W.H., Effects of Brief Relaxation Training on Autonomic Response to Anxiety—Evoking Stimuli. "Psychophysiology," 1974, 11:591-599.

Davidson, P.O. and Hiebert, S.F., Relaxation Training, Relaxation Instruction and Repeated Exposure to a Stressor Film. "Journal of Abnormal Psychology," 1971, 78:154-159.

Fenwick, P., The Neurophysiology of Meditation. "Intellectual Digest," November, 1973.

Gelhorn, E. and Kiely, W.F., Mystical States of Consciousness: Neurophysiological and Clinical Aspects. "Journal of Nervous and Mental Diseases," 1972, 154:399-405.

Gibbons, D., Hyperempiria, A New Altered State of Consciousness Induced by Suggestion. "Perceptual and Motor Skills," 1974, 39:47-53.

Goldfried, M.R., Systematic Desensitization as Training in Self-Control. "Journal of Consulting and Clinical Psychology," 1971, 37:228-234.

Goleman, D., Meditation as Meta-Therapy: Hypotheses Toward a Proposed Fifth State of Consciousness. "Journal of Transpersonal Psychology," 1971, 3:1-25.

Green, E.E., et al, Feedback Techniques for Deep Relaxation. "Psychophysiology," 1969, 6:371-377.

Kamiya, J., Conscious Control of Brainwaves. "Psychology Today," 1968, 1:57-60.

Lader, M. and Mathews, A., Comparison of Methods of Relaxation Using Physiological Measures. "Behaviour Research and Therapy," 1970, 8:331-337.

Lynch, J.J. and Paskewitz, D.A., On the Mechanisms of the Feedback Control of Human Brain Wave Activity. "Journal of Nervous and Mental Diseases," 1971, 153:205-217.

Marks, D.F., Individual Differences in the Vividness of Visual Imagery and Their Effects on Function. In P. Sheehan (ed.), "The Function and Nature of Imagery." New York: Academic Press, 1972.

Mathews, A.M. and Gelder, M.G., Psychophysiologic Investigations of Brief Relaxation Training, "Journal of Psychosomatic Research," 1969, 13:1-12.

Paul, G.L., Trimple, R.W., Recorded vs. 'Live' Relaxation Training and Hypnotic Suggestion: Comparative Effectiveness for Reducing Physiological Arousal and Inhibiting Stress Response. "Behavior Therapy," 1970, 1:285-302.

Paul, G.L., Physiological Effects of Relaxation Training and Hypnotic Suggestion. "Journal of Abnormal Psychology," 1969, 74:425-437.

Sarbin, T.R. and Juhasz, J.B., Toward a Theory of Imagination. "Journal of Personality," 1970, 38:52-76.

Shorr, J., "Psychoimagination Therapy: The Integration of Phenomenology and Imagination." New York: Intercontinental Medical Book Corp., 1972.

Chapter 9, Sleep and Dreaming.

Barber, T.X., Implications for Human Capabilities and Potentialities: Control of Dreaming. "Biofeedback and Self-Control 1974," 1975, 5:56-58.

Barber, T.X., Walker, P.C. and Hahn, K.W., Effects of Hypnotic Induction and Suggestions on Nocturnal Dreaming and Thinking. "Journal of Abnormal Psychology," 1973, 80:414.

Galigor, L., and May, R., "Dreams and Symbols: Man's Unconscious Language." New York: Basic Books, 1968.

Diamond, E., "The Science of Dreams." New York: Doubleday and Co., Inc., 1962.

Faraday, A., "Dream Power." New York: Coward, McCann and Geoghegan, 1972.

Faraday, A., "The Dream Game." New York: Harper and Row, Publisher, 1974.

Foulkes, D., "The Psychology of Sleep." New York: Charles Scribners's Sons, 1966.

Freeman, F.R., "Sleep Research: A Critical Review." Springfield, Ill.: Charles C. Thomas Publisher, 1972.

Garfield, P.L., "Creative Dreaming." New York: Simon and Schuster, 1974.

Garfield, P.L., Keeping a Longitudinal Dream Record. "Psychotherapy: Theory, Research, and Practice," 1973, 10:223-228.

Green, C., "Lucid Dreams." London: Hamilton, 1968.

Hall, C.S. and Nordby, V., "The Individual and His Dreams." New York: Signet Books, 1972.

Hartman, E., "The Biology of Dreaming." Springfield, Ill.: Charles C. Thomas, Publisher, 1967.

Hartmann, E., "Sleep and Dreaming." Boston: Little Brown and Company, 1970.

Hartmann, E., "The Function of Sleep." New Haven: Yale Univ. Press, 1973.

Hiscock, M., and Cohen, D., Visual Imagery and Dream Recall. "Journal of Research in Personality," 1973, 7:179-188.

Jones, R.M., "The New Psychology of Dreaming." New York: Grune and Stratton, 1970.

Jung, C.G., "Memories, Dreams, Reflections'" Aniela Jaffe (ed.). New York: Vintage, 1963.

Kramer, M., "Dream Psychology and the New Biology of Dreaming." Springfield, Ill.: Charles C. Thomas, Publisher, 1969.

Krippner, S., Ullman, M. and Vaughan, A., "Dream Telepathy." New York: MacMillan, 1973.

Luce, G.G., and Segal, J., "Sleep." New York: Lancer Books, Inc., 1967.

MacKenzie, N., "Dreams and Dreaming." London: Aldus Books, 1965.

Reed, H., Learning to Remember Dreams. "Journal of Humanistic Psychology," 1973, 13:33-48.

Rossi, E.L., "Dreams and the Growth of Personality." New York: Pergamon Press, 1972.

Sacerdote, P., "Induced Dreams." New York: Vantage Press, 1967.

Simon, C. and Emmons, W., Learning During Sleep? "Psychological Bulletin." 1955, 52:328-342.

Simon, C. and Emmons, W., Responses to Material Presented During Various Levels of Sleep. "Journal of Experimental Psychology," 1956, 51:89-97.

Tart, C.T. and Dick, L., Conscious Control of Dreaming: I. The Posthypnotic Dream. "Journal of Abnormal Psychology," 1970, 76:304-315.

Tart, C.T., Toward the Experimental Control of Dreaming: A Review of the Literature. "Psychological Bulletin," 1965, 64-88.

Van de Castle, R.L., "The Psychology of Dreaming." New York: General Learning Press, 1971.

Witkins, H.A., and Lewis, H.B., "Experimental Studies of Dreaming." New York: Random House, 1967.

Witkins, H.A., Influencing Dream Content. In M. Kramer (ed.) "Dream Psychology and the New Biology of Dreaming." Springfield, Ill.: Charles C. Thomas, Publihser, 1969.

Witkin, H.A., Presleep Experience and Dreams. In J. Fisher and L. Breger (eds.), "The Meaning of Dreams: Recent Insights from the Laboratory," (California Mental Health Research Symposium No. 3). Sacramento, Calif.

Chapter 10, Controlling Weight.

Bachrach, A.J., Erwin, W.J. and Mohr, J.P., The Control of Eating Behavior in an Anorexic by Operant Conditioning Techniques. L.Ullman and L. Krasner (eds.), "Case Studies in Behavior Modification." New York: Holt, Reinehart and Winston, 1965.

Bednar, R.L., Persuasibility and the Power of Belief. "Personnel and Guidance Journal," 1970, 48:647-652.

Brown, R.I., The Psychology of Obesity. "Physiotherapy," 1973, 59:216-218.

Cabanac, M., Physiological Role of Pleasure. "Science," 1971, 173:1103.

Goldiamond, I., Self-Control Procedures in Personal Behavior Problems. "Psychological Reports," 1965, 17:851-868.

Jeffery, D.B., A Comparison of the Effects of External Control and Self-Control on the Modification and Maintenance of Weight. "Journal of Abnormal Psychology," 1974, 83:404-410.

Salzman, L., Obsessive-Compulsive Aspects of Obesity. "Psychiatry in Medicine," 1972, 3:29-36.

Shipman, W.G. and Plesset, M.R., Anxiety and Depression in Obese Dieters. "Archives of General Psychiatry," 1963, 8:530-535.

Silverstone, J.T. and Solomon, T., The Long-Term Management of Obesity in General Practice. "British Journal of Clinical Practice," 1965, 19:395-398.

Slade, P.D., Experimental Investigations of Bodily Perception in Anorexia Nervosa and Obesity. "Psychotherapy and Psychosomatics," 1973, 22:359-363.

Stuart, R.B. and Davis, B., "Slim Chance in a Fat World: Behavioral Control of Obesity." Champaign, Ill.: Research Press, 1971.

Stunkard, A.J., Fox, S. and Levine, H., The Management of Obesity: Patient Self-Help and Medical Treatment. "Archives of Internal Medicine," 1970, 125:1067-1072.

Stunkard, A.J. and Burt, V., Obesity and the Body Image: II. Age at Onset of Disturbances in the Body Image. "American Journal of Psychiatry," 1967, 123: 1443-1447.

Chapter 11, Increasing Memory.

Bower, G.H., "The Psychology of Learning and Motivation: Advances in Research and Theory." New York: Academic Press, Inc., 1972.

Cole, G.H. and Gale, A., Physiological Reactivity as a Predictor of Performance in a Vigilance Task. "Psychophysiology," 1971, 8:584.

Dhanens, T.P., Hypnotic and Waking Suggestions and Recall. "International Journal of Experimental Hypnosis," 1975, 23:68-79.

Kondas, O., Reduction of Examination Anxiety and Stage-Fright by Group Desensitization and Relaxation. "Behavior Research and Therapy," 1967, 5:275-281.

Lahey, B.B., Facilitation of the Acquisition and Retention of Sight-Word Vocubulary Through Token Reinforcement. "Journal of Applied Behavior Analysis," 1974, 307-312.

Luborsky, L. and Blinder, B., Eye Fixation and Recall of Pictures as a Function of GSR (Galvanic Skin Response) Responsivity. "Perceptual Motor Skills," 1963, 16:469-483.

Rescorla, R.A. and Solomon, R.L., Two Process Learning Theory: Relationships Between Pavlovian Conditioning and Instrumental Learning. "Psychological Review," 1967, 74:151-182.

Schulman, R.E. and London, P., Hypnosis and Verbal Learning. "Journal of Abnormal and Social Psychology," 1963, 67:363-370.

Timmons, B.A., Delayed Auditory Feedback as a Factor Influencing Retention. "Perceptual and Motor Skills," 1974, 38:399-402.

Willemsen, E.W., The Effect of Affective Labeling of Response Items on Paired-Associates Learning. "Journal of General Psychology," 1973, 88:169-174.

Chapter 13, Stopping Pain.

Brown, R.A., Fader, K. and Barber, T.X., Responsiveness to Pain: Stimulus-Specificity Versus Generality. "Psychological Record," 1973, 23:1-7.

Budzynski, T.H., Stoyva, J.M. and Alder, C.S., EMG Biofeedback and Tension Headache: A Controlled Outcome Study. "Psychosomatic Mecicine," 1973, 35:484-496.

Chaves, J.F. and Barber, T.X., Cognitive Strategies, Experimenter Modeling and Expectation in the Attenuation of Pain. "Journal of Abnormal Psychology," 1974, 83:356-363.

Chaves, J.F. and Barber, T.X., Needles and Knives: Behind the Mystery of Acupuncture and Chinese Meridians. "Human Behavior," September, 1973, 19-24.

Chertok, L., "Psychosomatic Methods in Painless Childbirth." New York: Pergamon Press, 1959.

Davidson, P.O. and Neufeld, R.W.J., Response to Pain and Stress: A Multivariate Analysis. "Journal of Psychosomatic Research," 1974, 18:25-32.

Hilgard, E.R., Pain as a Puzzle for Psychology and Physiology. "American Psychologist," 1969, 24:103-113.

Johnson, R.F.Q., Suggestions for Pain Reduction and Response to Cold-Induced Pain. "Psychological Record," 1974, 24:161-169.

Melzack, R. and Perry, C., Self-Regulation of Pain: The Use of Alpha-Feedback and Hypnotic Training for the Control of Chronic Pain. "Experimental Neurology," 1975, 46:452.

Sacerdote, P., Theory and Practice of Pain Control in Malignancy and Other Protracted or Recurring Painful Illnesses. "International Journal of Clinical and Experimental Hypnosis." 1970, 18:160-168.

Sternback, R.A., "Pain: A Psychological Analysis." New York: Academic Press, 1968.

Wickramasekera, J.E., Temperature Feedback for the Control of Migraine. "Journal of Behavior Therapy and Experimental Psychiatry," 1973, 4:343-345.

Wolff, B.B., Factor Analysis of Human Pain Responses: Pain Endurance as a Specific Pain Factor. "Journal of Abnormal Psychology," 1971, 78:292-298.

Chapter 16, Lowering High Blood Pressure.

Brener, J., and Kleinmam, R.A., Learned Control of Decreases in Systolic Blood Pressure. "Nature," 1970, 226(170):1063.

Elder, S.T., et al, Instrumental Conditioning of Diastolic Blood Pressure in Essential Hypertensive Patients. "Journal of Applied Behavior Analysis," 1973, 6:377-382.

Henry, J.P. and Cassel, J.C., Psychosocial Factors in Essential Hypertension. Recent Epidemiologic and Animal Experimental Evidence. "American Journal of Epidemiology," 1969, 90:171-200.

Sapira, J.D., Scheib, E.T., Moriarity, R. and Shapiro, A.P., Dirrerences in Perception Between Hypertensive and Nonmotensive Populations. "Psychosomatic Medicine," 1971, 33:239-250.

Schwartz, G.E. and Shapiro, D., Biofeedback and Essential Hypertension: Current Findings and Theoretical Concerns. L. Birk (ed.), "Biofeedback: Behavioral Medicine." New York: Grune and Stratton, Inc., 1973.

Chapter 19, Decreasing Heart Attacks.

Friedman, M., "The Pathogensis of Coronary Artery Disease." New York: McGraw Hill Book Company, 1969.

Johnson, H.J. and Campos, J.J., The Effect of Cognitive Tasks and Verbalization Instructions on Heart Rate and Skin Conductance. "Psychophysiology," 1967, 4:143.

Lang, P.J., Sroufe, L.A. and Hastings, J.E., Effects of Feedback and Instructional Set on the Control of Cardiac-Rate Variability. "Journal of Experimental Psychology," 1967, 75:425-431.

Schwartz, G.E., Shaprio, D. and Tursky, B., Learned Control of Cardiovascular Integration in Man Through Operant Conditioning. "Psychosomatic Medicine," 1971, 33:57-62.

Scott, R.W., et al, A Shaping Procedure for Heart Rate Control in Chronic Tachycardia. "Perceptual and Motor Skills," 1973, 37:327-338.

Sutter, J.M. and Gerard, R., Psychic Factors in Cardiac Arrhythmias. "Union Medicale du Canada," 1968, 97:1055.

Troyer, W.G., et al, Learned Heart Rate Control in Patients with Ischemic Heart Disease. "Psychophysiology," 1973, 10:213.

Weiss, T. and Engel, B.T., Operant Conditioning of Heart Rate in Patients With Premature Ventricular Contractions. "Psychosomatic Medicine," 1971, 33:301-321.

Chapter 21, Controlling Other Diseases.

Barber, T.X., Implications for Human Capabilities and Potentialities: Control of Allergies. "Biofeedback and Self-Control 1974," 1975, 5:62-63.

Brandt, B., A Tentative Classification of Psychological Factors in the Etiology of Skin Diseases. "Journal of Investigative Dermatology," 1950, 14:81-90.

Holmes, T.H., Psychosocial and Psychophysiologic Studies of Tuberculosis. "Psychosomatic Medicine," 1967, 19:134-135.

Ikemi, Y., "Experimental Studies on the Psychosomatic Disorders of the Digestive System: Proceedings of the World Congress of Gastroenterology." Washington, D.C.: Williams and Wilkins Company, 1959.

Kiely, W.F., Stress and Somatic Disease. "Journal of the Americal Medical Association," 1973, 224:521.

LaBaw, W.L., Regular Use of Suggestibility by Pediatric Bleeders. "Haematologia," 1970, 4:419-425.

Maher-Loughnan, G.P., Emotional Aspects of Chest Diseases. "Geriatrics," 1971, 26:120-139.

Meyerowitz, S., The Continuing Investigation of Psychosocial Variables in Rheumatoid Arthritis. "Modern Trends in Rheumatology," 1971, 2:92-105.

Miller, N.E., Visceral Learning and Other Additional Facts Potentially Applicable to Psychotherapy. "International Psychiatric Clinics," 1969, 294-309.

Paley, A., Understanding the Psychologic Factors in Asthma. "Geriatrics," 1973, 28:54-62.

Rahe, R.H., Subjects Recent Life Changes and Their Near-future Illness Reports. "Annals of Clinical Research," 1971, 4:250-265.

Robbins, P.R., Personality and Psychosomatic Illness: A Selective Review of Research. "Genetic Psychology Monographs, 1969, 80:51-90.

Samuels, M. and Bennett, H., "The Well Body Book." New York: Random House-Bookworks, 1973.

Welgan, P.R., Learned Control of Gastric Acid Secretions in Ulcer Patients. "Psychosomatic Medicine," 1964, 36:411.

Wenger, M.A., Clemens, T.L. and Cullens, T.D., Autonomic Functions in Patients With Gastrointestinal and Dermatological Disorders. "Psychosomatic Medicine," 1962, 24:267-273.

Chapter 22, Stopping Fears and Phobias.

Bandura, A., Modelling Approaches to the Modification of Phobic Disorders. "Ciba Foundation Symposium: The Role of Learning in Psychotherapy." London: Churchill, 1968.

Dick-Read, J., "Childbirth Without Fear." New York: Harper & Row Publishers, 1953.

Frankel, F.H., Trance Capacity and the Genesis of Phobic Behavior. "Archives of General Psychiatry," 1974, 31:261-263.

Garfield, Z., et al, Effect of 'In Vivo' Training on Experimental Desensitization of a Phobia. "Psychological Reports," 1967, 20:515-519.

Hussain, M.Z., Desensitization and Flooding in Treatment of Phobias. "American Journal of Psychiatry," 1971, 127:1509.

McGlynn, F.D. and Williams, C.W., Systematic Desensitization of Snake Avoidance Under Three Conditions of Suggestion. "Journal of Behavior Therapy and Experimental Psychiatry," 1970, 1:97.

Rachman, S., "Phobias: Their Nature and Control." Springfield, Ill.: Charles C. Thomas, 1968.

Chapter 23, Overcoming Alcohol and Drugs.

Bigelow, G., Alcoholic Drinking: Suppression by a Brief Time-Out Procedure. "Behavior Research and Therapy," 1974, 12:107-115.

Griffiths, R., Suppression of Ethanol Self-Administration in Alcoholics by Contingent Time-Out From Social Interactions. "Behavior Research and Therapy," 1974, 12:327-334.

Kurtz, P.S., Treating Chemical Dependency Through Biofeedback. "Hospital Progress," 1974. 55:68.

Maletzky, B.M., Assisted Covert Sensitization for Drug Abuse. "International Journal of the Addictions," 1974, 9:411-429.

Martin, R.D., Reduction of Adolescent Drug Abuse Through Post-Hypnotic Association. "Canadian Counsellor," 1974, 8:211-216.

Chapter 24, Increasing Sexual Responsiveness.

Dengrove, E., Behavior Therapy of the Sexual Disorders. "Journal of Sexual Research," 1967, 49-61.

Dengrove, E., The Mechanotherapy of Sexual Disorders. "Journal of Sexual Research," 1971, 7:1-12.

Gellhorn, E. and Loofbourrow, G.N., "Emothions and Emotional Disorders." New York: Harper and Row, Publishers, 1963.

Green, R., "Sexual Conflict in Children and Adults." New York: Basic Books, 1974.

Kraft, T., Behavior Therapy and the Treatment of Sexual Perversions. "Psychotherapy and Psychosomatics," 1967, 15:351-357.

Lidberg, L., Social and Psychiatric Aspects of Impotence and Premature Ejaculation. "Archives of Sexual Behavior," 1972, 2:135-146.

Masters, W.H. and Johnson, V.E., "Human Sexual Response." Boston: Little, Brown, 1966.

Otto, H.A., "Counseling in Marital and Sexual Problems." Baltimore: Williams and Wilkins, 1965.

Rachman, S., Sexual Disorders and Behavior Therapy. "American Journal of Psychiatry," 1961, 118:235.

Renshaw, D.C., Sexuality and Depression in Adults and the Elderly. "Medical Aspects of Human Sexuality," 1975, 9:40-62.

Stuart, R.B., Operant Interpersonal Treatment for Martial Discord. "Journal of Consulting and Clinical Psychology," 1969, 33:675.

Watson, D. and Baumal, E., Effects of Locus of Control and Expectation of Future Control Upon Present Performance. "Journal of Personality and Social Psychology," 1967, 212-215.

Weiss, H.D., The Physiology of Human Penile Erection. "Annals of Internal Medicine," 1972, 76:703.

Chapter 25, Achieving Emotional Stability.

Alexander, L., Mind and Body in Biological Psychiatry. "Biological Psychiatry," 1972, 12:225-238.

Buck, R.W., Class Method in Treatment of Essential Hypertension. "Annals of Internal Medicine," 1937, 11:511-578.

Davison, G. and Valins, S., On Self-Produced and Drug-Produced Relaxation. "Behavior Research and Therapy," 1968, 6:401-402.

Frankel, V.E., "Man's Search for Meaning: An Introduction to Logotherapy." New York: Washington Square Press, 1969, 172:173-175.

Fuller, R.B., "Utopia or Oblivion: The Prospects for Humanity." New York: Bantam Books, Inc., 1969.

Gabor, D., "The Mature Society." London: Secker and Warbury, 1972.

Gellhorn, E. and Kiely, W.F., "Biological Psychiatry." New York: John Wiley and Sons, 1973.

Goldfried, M.R., Effectiveness of Relaxation as an Active Coping Skill. "Journal of Abnormal Psychology," 1974, 83:348-355.

Hart, J.T., Autocontrol of EEG Alpha. "Psychophysiology," 1968, 5:506.

Jacobson, E. "Anxiety and Tension Control." Philadelphia: J.B. Lippincott Company, 1964.

Johnson, D.T. and Spielberger, C.D., The Effects of Relaxation Training and the Passage of Time on Measures of State and Trait Anxiety. "Journal of Clinical Psychology," 1968, 24:20-23.

Nideffer, R.M., Alpha and the Development of Human Potential. "Biofeedback and Self-Control 1971," 1973, 167-188.

Oziel, L.J., Effects of Feedback on Self-Reinforcing Behavior in Relation to Self-Acceptance. "Psychological Reports," 1974, 34:1039-1044.

Paul, G.L., Extraversion, Emotionality and Physiological Response to Relaxation Training and Hypnotic Suggestion. "International Journal of Clinical and Experimental Hypnosis," 1969, 17:88-89.

Raskin, M., Johnson, G. and Rondestvedt, J.W., Chronic Anxiety Treated by Feedback Induced Muscle Relaxation. "Archives of General Psychiatry," 1973. 28:263-267.

Schmeidler, G. and Lewis, L., Mood Changes After Alpha Feedback Training. "Perceptual and Motor Skills," 1971 32:709-710.

Suinn, R.M. and Hall, R., Marathon Desensitization Groups. "Behavior Research and Therapy," 1970, 8:97-98.

Winett, R.A., Group Feedback and Group Contigencies in Modifying Behavior of Fifth Graders. "Psychological Reports," 1974, 34:1283-1292.

Chapter 26, *Extrasensory Perception.*

Bolen, J.G., Profiles in Business: Top Executives Disclose ESP. "Psychic Magazine, December 1974.

Brand, W.G. and Brand, L.W., Preliminary Explorations of Psi-Conducive States: Progressive Muscular Relaxation. "Journal of the American Society for Psychical Research," 1973, 67:26-46.

Cavanna, R (ed.), "Psi-favorable States of Consciousness: Proceedings of an International Converence on Methodology in Psi Research." New York: Parapsychology Foundation, 1970.

Chari, C.T.K., Psychophysiological Issues About EEG Alpha Activity and ESP. "Journal of the American Society for Psychical Research," 1970 64:411-420.

Dixon, N.F., "Subliminal Perception: The Nature of a Controversy." New York: McGraw Hill, 1971.

Hornton, C., Significant Factors in Hypnotically-Induced Clairvoyant Dreams. "Journal of the American Society for Psychical Research," 1972, 66:86-102.

James, W., "William James in Psychical Research." New York: The Viking Press, 1963.

Jung, C.G., Synchronicity: An Acausal Connecting Principle." New York: Pantheon, 1955.

Koestler, A., "The Roots of Coincidence." London: Hutchinson, 1972.

Kreskin, "The Amazing World of Kreskin." New York: Random House, 1973.

Krippner, S. and Rubin, D. (eds.), "Galaxies of Light."
New York: Doubleday, 1973.

Murphy, G., "The Challenge of Psychical Research."
New York: Harper and Brothers, 1961.

Porter, J., "Psychic Development." New York: Random
House-Bookworks, 1974.

Rhine, J.B., "ESP." Boston: Bruce Humphries, 1964.

Ullman, M., An Experimental Approach to Dreams and
Telepathy: Methodology and Preliminary Findings. "Archives
of General Psychiatry," 1966, 14:605-613.

Ullman, M., Krippner, S. and Vaughan, A., "Dream
Telepathy."New York: MacMillan, 1973.

Van De Castle, R.L., The Facilitation of ESP Through
Hypnosis. " American Journal of Clinical Hypnosis," 1969,
12:37-56.

Chapter 29, *Enhancing Religious Experiences.*

Barton, R.T., "Religious Doctrine and Medical Practice."
Springfield, Ill.: Charles C. Thomas, Publisher, 1958.

Bryan, W.J., "Religious Aspects of Hypnosis." Springfield, Ill.: Charles C. Thomas, Publisher, 1962.

Dobzhansky, T.G., "The Biology of Ultimate Concern."
New York: New American Library, 1967.

Ikemi, Y., The Biologic Wisdom of Self-Regulatory Mech-
anism of Normalization in Autogenic and Oriental Approaches in Psychotherapy. "Psychotherapy and Psycho-
matics," 1975, 25:99-108.

Wittkofski, J.N., "The Pastoral Use of Hypnotic Technique."
New York: The Macmillan Company, 1961.

TOTAL MIND POWER—PROGRESS CHART

Goal to attain or,
Problem to resolve_____

	Mon.	Tues.	Wed.
First Week			
Second Week			
Third Week			
Succeeding Weeks:			

Under Monday of the first week, make a brief note
of your current situation/condition to be improved.
Note and record your progress daily or weekly as
you apply your Total Mind Power.

Thurs.   Fri.   Sat.   Sun.

INDEX